When God Shuts The Lion's Mouth

I0417978

A Message of Deliverance to the Children of God!

Pastors/Missionaries Joe & Joey Serda
Write To:
Word of God Bible Ministries
Publishing Division
P O Box 1346, Anderson, MO. 64831

All scripture references taken from the
King James Version of the Bible.

Printed by DiggyPOD, Inc., in the United States of America.

First printing, 2022

ISBN: 979-8-9858435-0-7 (Paperback)

Word of God Bible Ministries/Publishing Division
P O Box 1346
Anderson, MO. 64831
Email To: wogbmjoey@gmail.com
Ph#417-223-2793

We dedicate this work to our Lord Jesus Christ, for His abundant grace and love toward us: and to His church, for the encouragement of our faithful brothers and sisters in Jesus!
And to my wife Joey, for her love, prayers, and strength in the Lord!

For Prayer, Ministry CD's, Meetings or more information call #417-223-2793

TABLE OF CONTENTS

Introduction and Theme . . .

This journey of life's sea has many unexpected perils and dangers. Many times situations that come our way are so unforeseeable and unpredictable. As the seas can become unstable, and uncontrollable, so become the trials and testing times in this life for the child of God.

As our faith and trust grows more dependent upon the Lord Jesus, we will find ourselves many times faced with an enemy that rages against us, to try to destroy that faith that we have in the living God, and His Son Jesus Christ. We as children of the Lord, whether laymen or His minister's, are tried many times beyond limits that we never knew existed: sometimes in dark days of heartache, sorrow, trouble and anguish. These situations seem to come especially to those who are called into places of ministry and leadership: The enemy attacks the leadership first before the body, to bring down his prey.

As we near the coming of the Lord and see the ever rising tide that flows against the church and the Lord's ministers, we realize more and more that our adversary the devil, is come with all force; death and hell following. With no mercy, no feeling, and certainly no remorse, his ultimate goal is to destroy every soul that he can, and cause the great havoc that we see in the perils of today's society. Sin, sickness, disease, civil unrest in our communities, racial conflicts, broken homes, drug addiction, alcohol abuse, child abuse; the list goes on and on. Satan is a terrible paymaster. His chains of deceptive darkness seek to capture lives and bring them into captivity: having no respect he reaches into the homes and lives of countless souls, even in Christian homes. Is there something that can be done to stop the death and destruction that is brought about by such a ruthless enemy? In the following pages, we will search to find the answer to this question in the pages of the Holy Scriptures. The Lord has an answer to help us to be the overcoming church that He is coming back for. And in the end, we know that we will have our victory over our adversary. He is a defeated foe through the precious blood of Jesus Christ our Lord! Open your heart to receive this message of power and eternal hope we have in Him!

"Be sober, be vigilant; because your adversary the devil, as a <u>roaring lion</u>, walketh about, seeking whom he may devour: (1 Peter 5:8KJV)

This will be the scripture theme of this study: This is the place where the child of God meets the ever prideful roar of an enemy that would like to destroy us. The roar of our spiritual adversary, the devil, rages against us in this life, many times intimidating and fierce, attempting to cause us to bow in fear to the endless struggle of spiritual warfare. As a child of God, our battles can many times seem unending, and very difficult to overcome. Daily struggles to conquer this adversary seem to go on and on, with no help or reprieve from this kind of torment. Whether young or old, rich or poor; whatever place we hold in today's society, we are never exempt from the roar of the adversary that would like to destroy us if possible. Temptation's sting is always present to cause us to falter and fail if possible, and the burden of condemnation and accusation follows not far behind. If possible, he would like to destroy God's elect, and bring havoc to the body of Christ. As to the shepherds of the sheep, the great burden and responsibility of caring for the flock is an unending task. Sleepless nights, and weariness of mind is one of the greatest tools the enemy would like to use against us. As this scripture tells us, he walks about, seeking whom he may devour: This is a truthful fact that we cannot avoid. In the life of ministry, and as a child of God, Satan's desire is to sift us, and destroy us if possible. That would be his greatest trophy. As Jesus told Simon Peter, **"Simon, Simon, behold, Satan hath desired to have you, that he may sift you as wheat:"** That word "sift" in the Greek means to "riddle". That is to utter destruction, with no chance of coming back. But that's when the Lord reassured Peter and said, *"But I have prayed for thee, that thy faith fail not: and when thou art converted, strengthen thy brethren. (Luke 22:31-32)* Now is the task given to us, to fight the good fight of faith, to finish our course: to keep the faith, and encourage those around us, because Jesus is praying for us! Our wonderful High Priest that can be touched with the feeling of our infirmities, *(Hebrews 4:15)* is ever pleading our cause and will deliver us out of the mouth of the Lion!

As you begin to read this study, open your heart to the Lord's power of deliverance, knowing that He is faithful to give us power over all the power of the enemy, the devil. No matter how loud he roars, Jesus still gives us the victory! Praise the Lord forever!

Pastors Joe and Joey Serda

CHAPTER ONE:

PAUL THE APOSTLE –DEFENDER OF THE GOSPEL

"I am set for the defense of the gospel." (Phil.1:17)

We're going to begin our study in chapter four of the book of second Timothy; a very familiar scripture we have read many times. Paul the apostle is one of the great examples we can read of: his life, his testimony, and the inspiration he was to those he saw converted, as he reached them with the power of the Gospel. We know the Lord used him mightily to pen a good part of the New Testament, as he was moved by the Holy Ghost.

When thinking of Paul the apostle, we know he learned many things throughout his life in ministry; and I'm sure he would testify to us that it was a great journey. He could probably say he never expected to be called to be a minister of the Gospel of Jesus Christ, because of his past life in persecuting the church, not feeling worthy of the Lord and his great calling. There are many pastors, preachers, and holy leaders the Lord has given us today, and they can testify of the situations they have encountered in ministry, even as Paul the apostle. Maybe feeling they would never have been worthy to be called into the ministry, or to experience the things they have been thru in the ministry, but still can testify that ministry has been a great journey, and the Lord has been faithful every step of the way. The Lord has been the keeper, as he kept Paul the apostle, until the day that he was going to receive his reward. Even so we now must also prepare our hearts to endure, and fight the good fight of faith unto the end.

We're going to do our best to bring this message to you, as we feel it in our hearts. We pray it will help us to prepare so we might be the vessels to carry this great Gospel through our lifetime, and help others to continue on this journey. Let us look to the scripture:

2 Timothy 4:6-18:

6) *For I am now ready to be offered, and the time of my departure is at hand.*

7) *I have fought a good fight, I have finished my course, I have kept the faith:*

8) *Henceforth there is laid up for me a crown of righteousness, which the Lord, the righteous judge, shall give me at that day: and not to me only, but unto all them also that love his appearing.*

9) *Do thy diligence to come shortly unto me:*

10) *For Demas hath forsaken me, having loved this present world, and is departed unto Thessalonica; Crescens to Galatia, Titus unto Dalmatia.*

11) *Only Luke is with me. Take Mark, and bring him with thee: for he is profitable to me for the ministry.*

12) *And Tychicus have I sent to Ephesus.*

13) *The cloke that I left at Troas with Carpus, when thou comest, bring **with thee**, and the books, but especially the parchments.*

14) *Alexander the coppersmith did me much evil:*

the Lord reward him according to his works:

15) Of whom be thou ware also; for he hath greatly withstood our words.

*16) At my first answer no man stood with me, but all **men** forsook me: **I pray God** that it may not be laid to their charge.*

*17) Notwithstanding the Lord stood with me, and strengthened me; that by me the preaching might be fully known, and **that** all the Gentiles might hear: and I was delivered out of the mouth of the lion.*

*18) And the Lord shall deliver me from every evil work, and will preserve **me** unto his heavenly kingdom: to whom **be** glory for ever and ever. Amen.*

We thank the Lord for His written word, for every word that proceedeth out of the mouth of God! As for Paul the apostle, we can understand there were many trials he faced after his conversion. From the time the Lord Jesus sent Ananias to pray for him, he told Ananias, **(*Act 9:16) "For I will shew him how great things he must suffer for my name's sake."*** This was the beginning of that great journey of ministry for Paul. Many things were set in order and set in motion from God's divine providence: Paul was going to experience, and he was going to have to go through extreme suffering and persecution. We can gain from him as a great example, as he was willing to not only stand through the test, but stand faithful to the call of

God in his life. Paul was a great example of that steadfast faith. He had many obstacles and many enemies, from town to town and place to place, there was always something the enemy would put in his way as a great hindrance. To hinder his walk with God, to hinder his ministry and what he had been called to do. But Paul realized he could depend upon the promises of God! He could depend upon the living Word of God! He could depend upon the written Word of God! As we behold this beautiful testament he was writing unto Timothy his son in the faith, let us understand that he was giving instruction to him, letting him know of things that would come his way in ministry. Timothy, being a young man in the faith and in the walk with God, called to ministry, truly needed Paul to encourage him. He wanted to teach Timothy that He could count on what the Lord spoke, and what the Lord had promised to him.

Even so, now there may be many things in our lives today that we may be facing as this young man would. Things we thought we would never see in our life time, or have to deal with. We know the coming of the Lord is near, and we've always believed that the Lord Jesus would come and get us out this world, and not have to experience different struggles in this life. But there is something we can see here through the life of Paul the apostle that we can apply to our lives. He could have been very well shaken in his faith. Maybe he could have even felt discouraged, or disheartened by the way he had been abandoned by those he cared about; he probably felt abandoned and mistreated. But thank God, he was holding onto the one that could keep him and preserve him through the thick and thin, regardless of the obstacle; regardless of the trial; regardless of the test. There was something about this man that he knew he could stand upon the promises of God.

Can we just thank God for his promises, that they are ever true, they are ever faithful?! We can sing the glory of his promises because he never fails, and He will fulfill them to everyone that believes upon Him! Paul was a great example; he not only trusted, depended, and confided in the Lord, but he made the written word of God his life, no matter what came his way. Even as the adversary, walking about him as a roaring lion, wanted to devour and destroy him. But he still trusted in the Lord's promise. In the presence and spirit of God, he knew the Holy Ghost would preserve him and keep him unto the day of the glorious appearing of the Lord Jesus. Are you relying upon him today? Are you trusting in the Lord's unchanging word? Are you confiding in His everlasting presence? Are you holding on to His promises, that cannot be compared to the material, the natural, and that will never pass away? We are not living by bread alone, or by the natural things of this life. We don't live by what we can feel, see, or touch with our natural senses. We walk by faith and not by sight. The just shall live by faith, and we must live by the faith we have in the Word of God!

We now come to our scripture theme; *"When God Shuts the Lion's Mouth"*. There are many times through the years that we have been faced by a lion; by an adversary; by an enemy. The devices and the wiles of the devil many times go even beyond our imagination. The display of sin and evil that is going on around us is many times unbelievable. The fight and fierce roar of the enemy and his tactics are incredibly terrible and terrifying to the root, and can cause us to lose our faith, if we don't hold on to the Lord with all that we have. As we now can see how things are unfolding before our very eyes; Bible prophecy is being fulfilled as the revealing of sin is shocking, and is all around us. We now realize how close to the end we truly are.

What would cause people to go into our city streets and begin to tear and beat down business buildings, breaking glass and setting fire to those places? We are seeing a full display of the sinful nature of man that is coming to life and being displayed in so many different ways. The adversary is roaring openly against the truth and against God's people. It is sometimes unbelievable; the destructive force of an enemy whose roar wants to ravage the very faith and hope that we have in the living God. What can it be to cause even our government to turn to control tactics, and domination of free citizen's lives? They are now seeking to destroy the faith we have in God's word the Bible. When our nation that was founded on prayer, the Bible, the Christian walk and our Savior Jesus Christ, and is now turning to the godless, humanistic ideals of this 21st century?! Even now they are tearing the Bible to pieces, doing anything they can to pass laws contrary to the Lord's commands. The scriptures of God's holy word are regarded as nothing, and being torn apart, while old and young alike are rejecting the Lord and his great plan of salvation. The young generation has given in to the roar of the devil himself and desiring socialistic sinful ways of life that only deceive and destroy.

It can bring tears to our eyes and agony to our souls to see our great land falling apart into shambles. It breaks our hearts to see people reject the Lord, and His great salvation, and turn to the godless ways of the unregenerate. We are moved to a point of hopelessness, as people's hearts are being hardened by this deceptive enemy that roars against God's shepherds and their flocks. We can understand by Paul's writings to Timothy that there was something burdening his heart. He was joyful in that he was making his journey towards glory, but yet he was troubled and in agony because of the experiences he had with those around him. He knew the adversary was working in the lives of God's people, seeking to destroy them. He realized the enemy would do anything it would take to destroy the church if he could. We must take notice at this point and realize that as the conflict gets stronger, and as our standards are challenged, our faith is put to the test. The battle is raging and the devil is roaring to a point where it seems it is getting worse rather than better: we are just about to reach our greatest victory in Christ Jesus! When we feel the pressure all around us, and trouble oppressing our soul, can we remember that *"greater is he that is in you, than he that is in the world."*(1John 4:4) Can we remember to not be *"weary in our well doing; for in due season we shall reap if we faint not."* (Galatians 6:9) Paul was trying to urge Timothy, and he greatly expressed to him the urgency of preparing himself for these kinds of battles. Paul was feeling some broken heartedness, in knowing that there had been some loss. He also had a longing and desire that the Lord would have mercy to redeem those he loved in the faith out of the mouth of the lion.

He spoke of Demas, that he had forsaken him, loving the present world. Was it possible that Demas had gone off on the wrong path, and lost his way from the truth? Or, as some believe that he was afraid to lose his life to martyrdom, as many of the apostles did. But Paul felt some loss and sadness concerning Demas. As pastors, we know the feeling of having a sheep go astray; knowing that the ever present evil of temptation is working to destroy the souls of men, and only the Lord can spare that soul from destruction that is inevitable if they don't repent and turn back to Jesus. Jesus spoke of his shepherds as those that "leave the ninety-nine, to seek the one": to find that one that has gone the wrong direction. How many times in the life and ministry of Paul the apostle, though he was a great man of God, he still was moved by the burden and love for God's people. So much that it broke his heart when one would go astray. The scripture says that he carried *"the care of all the churches". (2 Corinthians 11:28)* He knew the devil was bringing havoc upon many of the church. It was not only through persecution, but by pulling on their faith to destroy their walk with the Lord; tearing lives apart and destroying those that once lived for God, and depended upon his holy Word.

Even now, in this day, when this pandemic situation has caused many churches to have to close their services, we have heard from many pastors that are concerned about their flocks. They have become comfortable as sheep not having the fellowship of the flock, and the feeding of the shepherd. One pastor told us his congregation is falling apart, and losing their desire to come to church, because of the government shutdowns, and the limiting of congregations because of this plague and sickness. They aren't able to have revivals because of the attendance. The souls are dying, and not able to get into the presence of the Lord. All of the social distancing and talk of death is putting fear into the hearts of the American church, and taking away our experience with the Lord. This lion is certainly roaring loud, using the news media to destroy the faith of God's people. Many churches have resorted to online services, and what is called virtual church. An online experience in church is okay, but we need the fellowship of the presence of the Lord and His people. It's time to prepare for heaven, not to stray away and grow cold in him. There is no time to become complacent and comfortable staying home, and feeling that having church at home is enough when there is an adversary that is out to destroy my soul and yours! We can't give in to his tactics to take away our freedom of worshipping the Lord freely! There is no virus, sickness, disease, or sin that can stand against the God we serve, and He will give us the victory over all. If I allow the devil to take my soul, my salvation, my victory, and my healing from the Lord, he will do it gladly! We must stand up and fight for what is ours from the Lord. His word is His display to us how much he loves us and wants to save us, and keep us unto the great day of his second coming! He knows how to put the enemy to flight, and shut the lion's mouth! He can stop him in his tracks, because the devil doesn't have his foot on the neck of the church. Oh no! We know the glorious Savior that holds the keys to death, hell and the grave! His name is Jesus! His name is Jesus! Call upon his wonderful name! There is power in his name! His name is the living Word of God, and He is coming back in truth and in righteousness to bring judgment one of these days very soon! Jude says, ***"The Lord cometh with ten thousand of his saints"*** (Jude 1:14), and we need to be looking for him, rather than letting this cowardly enemy steal the victory from our souls and from our sheep. When the saints go marching in, we've got to be in that number!

The greatest struggle will take place just before the final victory! Paul had made his journey, he had kept the faith. He told Timothy, "I have fought a good fight". It is a great fight, but it's a good fight. It's a fight worth fighting for! It will be worth it all when we see Jesus! Every bruise, every wound, every bump on my head, every kick, every stumble, will be worth it all! It may hurt, but it will be well worth the journey. This enemy may try to cause me to fall, but we must jump right back up and keep running. Why? Because we know in whom we have believed, and He is able to keep that which have committed unto him against that great day! Are you persuaded that the Lord can keep you, and help you to overcome this terrible enemy that would like to destroy us? He is faithful to deliver those that will cry out to him, and believe him for that great deliverance. He is in control of all things, and there is no adversary, nor his devices that will be able to trouble us, because our

Lord fights for us. He will shut the lions' mouth! He knows how to shut the lion's mouth!

Paul spoke of another lion that was roaring against him. He said, *"Alexander the coppersmith did me much evil: the Lord reward him according to his works." (Verse 14)* This man was an enemy in the flesh sent to hinder the apostle any way he could. Because of Paul's preaching and stand for the Lord, souls were being delivered from the plague of sinful idolatry, and the worship of false gods. But still, Paul preached on and didn't allow the sufferings of the flesh to stop him from the call of God upon his life. Even so we must do, and continue to obey the Lord in the face of persecution, whether spiritual or physical. The reward will greatly outweigh the sufferings of this present time. Paul taught that to the Romans in chapter 8, verse 18: *"For I reckon that the sufferings of this present time are not worthy to be compared with the glory which shall be revealed in us."* His confidence was in this promise the Lord gave to him.

Sadly, Paul had to state that at his first answer *"no man stood with me"* (verse 16). Paul had to stand before the emperor of Rome, Nero, twice as history records. And when he did, he testified to Timothy that no one stood with him to take his part. No one came to his defense, to help plead for him. No one was there to witness in his behalf. The entire Roman court, the emperor, the devil, they were all against him. It probably seemed that the whole world was against him.

Many times we can feel that the whole world is against us. Many times we can feel outnumbered, that we are walking a lonesome valley by ourselves. But Paul, with that deep inward strength of the Holy Ghost, that power that didn't come by his own abilities, but only the power of the Holy Ghost within him raised up to the fight. That's what a powerful prayer life can do in the life of a child of God! The beauty of hearing glorious prayers in other tongues going up to heaven, in that beautiful heavenly language; the glorious evidence of the gift of the Holy Ghost, it brings us to a place of true victory. We love to hear people praying in the Holy Ghost, worshipping the Lord! That's what we need in this day and time so desperately! Oh Lord, send the power just now! The time comes when we must allow that inward strength of the Holy Ghost to rise up within us, and help us to overcome. He begins to stand and comfort us, and as the Comforter he lets us know it is possible to win the victory over this ruthless spiritual enemy. That power comes from on high, and helps me to overcome the power of the adversary. Brother and Sister, it will not be in vain; every prayer, every praise! The Lord honors them all, and receives them all. There are times we become weary; the flesh doesn't want to go through, doesn't want to do what is necessary to bring true victory. It may be a push and a struggle, but at the end of this journey, it will be worth it all!

Paul declared it, he said even though no one stood with him, but that all forsook him. He said, *"Notwithstanding the Lord stood with me, and strengthened me!" (v.17)* PRAISE GOD! The Lord not only stands with us through our trials but he dwells within us. He fills our souls, and takes this earthly vessel to use for his glory and his honor. It's such a great honor for the Holy Ghost to use our life, and for someone that will declare "I'm not alone, I know the Lord is with me and will help me, He will do it!" I know He's fighting for me, He's going before me, every step that I take; He's preparing it before me! Even if the devil tries to trip me and make me fall, I'm standing upon the unchanging promises of the Lord. Repeating again, Paul said the Lord stood with him; He had someone greater than the emperor of Rome, someone that had all power in his mighty hand: His name is Jesus! Just glorify him right now where you are! Jesus! Jesus! He promised that He would never leave us nor forsake us. He said, "Lo I am with you always, even unto the end of the world", and He will not fail. He is with you, and his great expression of character has been shown through your life. There is no question why the devil rages as a roaring lion against you, to destroy you if possible?

The Lord Jesus shows himself to be with us at all times. He not only stands with us, he strengthens us.

This is why in this day of perilous times, we must be confident that the Lord will not allow us to fall prey to this enemy that is raging against us: even when he comes in the form of sickness and affliction. We will say this, many have been troubled about the virus that has been sweeping across the nation and world, and for health sake have been very cautious. But we must be encouraged, and know that the Lord is our protection. For it is written! Exodus 23:25 says, *"I will take sickness away from the midst of thee".* *Dueteronomy 7:15 says, "The Lord will take away from thee all sickness".* That word all covers everything and nothing is excluded. He declared to the children of Israel that he was their *"Jehovah-Raphah", which means "I am the Lord that healeth thee". (Exodus 15:26)* That is the living Word of GOD! We know that we are the church that believes the Word of God, so just believe it!

Let us believe the Word of God that *"no plague should come nigh our dwelling". (Psalm 91:10)* This body may be frail, and weak at times, and many times that lion roars against us with sickness. But when we believe the Word of God, it fights every battle for us, and we can count on what His promise says. We have known enough great saints of God that loved the Lord with all their heart, like Paul the apostle, and many others, that dedicated their lives to the Lord and ministry. And when it came time for them to leave this life, the Lord gave their request, and blessed them by carrying them home to glory. Death hurts and death is painful, but their eyes were on glory, and the glimpse of Jesus on the other side.

We would like to encourage you, don't allow any fear to trouble you. There's a mouth of a lion that roars every day, through everyday situations, in the news media, the newspapers, on the radio, everywhere you turn and everywhere you see and hear him roaring, and seeking whom he may devour. The Lord spoke it by the mouth of Paul, *"that by me the preaching might be fully known; that all the Gentiles might hear: and I was delivered out of the mouth of the Lion."* (Verse 17) No one could deliver him: only the Lord. Truthfully, we are at the point in life now where only the Lord can keep us, only He can help us, and deliver us. Only he can preserve us and keep us from all evil, temptation, and the roaring of the devil that roars against us. Thank the Lord that He has given us examples of faith, so that we can be encouraged to listen and receive instruction to be able to overcome.

We would like to tell you that there are unseen divine preparations being made right now to help us in this great journey of life. They are unseen and unknown to us, but are being made right now for us in glory:

the Lord himself that will fight the battle for us when the lion roars against us. The defense has been set in place, the artillery made available, the power of God is behind us, and Jesus is going before us preparing the way. Thank God that we can count on that Wonderful, Counselor; our Prince of Peace! He is the one that gives me peace of mind when my mind is so troubled by the unending roars of the adversary. When I'm so confused with all that I see and hear, then comes my Prince of Peace, Jesus! He is making preparation for me and you, as we are fretting with impatience. When we are hungry, he gives us manna to eat. When we are thirsty, he gives us living water to drink. When we are perplexed on every side, remember; *"the angel of the Lord encampeth round about them that fear him, and delivereth them." (Psalm 34:7)*

Paul could have been shaken by the many things that came against him in his life of ministry, but we can appreciate a man of God that took a stand, and stood upon the Word of God. There may be a lion, an adversary roaring against you. But the Lord knows how to shut his mouth! You may be in a valley of stern conflict now, but your life is in His hands. He knows how to put a stop to the devil, and tell him it's enough! He will stop him in his tracks! Satan has to flee, and be cast out, because he can't stay when Jesus is there. Jesus' blood will deliver you. When you feel like your rope of hope is about to break and your faith is about to fail, look up to Jesus: reach beyond the visible, and seek His hand in the invisible. The scripture says in *2 Corinthians 4:18: "While we look not at the things which are seen, but at the things which are not seen: for the things which are seen are temporal; but the things which are not seen are eternal."* Hold on to His unchanging hand, and seek His mercy and His grace!

"And when they were come to him, he said unto them, Ye know, from the first day that I came into Asia, after what manner I have been with you at all seasons, Serving the Lord with all humility of mind, and with many tears, and temptations, which befell me by the lying in wait of the Jews: And how I kept back nothing that was profitable unto you, but have shewed you, and have taught you publickly, and from house to house, Testifying both to the Jews, and also to the Greeks, repentance toward God, and faith toward our Lord Jesus Christ. And now, behold, I go bound in the spirit unto Jerusalem, not knowing the things that shall befall me there: Save that the Holy Ghost witnesseth in every city, saying that bonds and afflictions abide me. But none of these things move me, neither count I my life dear unto myself, so that I might finish my course with joy, and the ministry, which I have received of the Lord Jesus, to testify the gospel of the grace of God."

(Acts 20:18-24)

CHAPTER TWO:
DAVID – THE SHEPERD BOY MADE KING

"I have found David the son of Jesse, a man after mine own heart, which shall fulfil all my will." (Acts 13:22)

As we begin our second chapter, we will continue our theme as we journey into the lives of other biblical characters that were challenged by the enemy. A savage enemy, that would not spare to destroy a child of the Lord within his reach. We have spoken much about this enemy, the devil, as he roars against those called by the Lord, and the subtle devices he uses to destroy. Still, we continue to see, that in the face of this enemy that roars as a lion, we still have a way of deliverance: we have our great and mighty Savior Jesus Christ who delivers us out of his mouth!

We have much to share with you concerning the life of a young shepherd boy called by God, who is not unfamiliar to us. The Lord had a special call for David, as he in his youth was being prepared for great things. Scripture records to us the glorious testimony of what the Lord prepared in David's life:

Psalm 78:70-72 says, "He chose David also his servant, and took him from the sheepfolds: From following the ewes great with young he brought him to feed Jacob his people, and Israel his inheritance. So he fed them according to the integrity of his heart; and guided them by the skilfulness of his hands."

Even now, to you that are reading this writing, the Lord is calling you to something special; a calling whose shoes none other can fill. Even now you may be walking in that calling, and doing all you can to fulfill the task laid before you. So let us take these great examples given to us in the Word of God, and allow the spirit of the Lord to prepare and shape our lives as we open our hearts to Him. Whatever the calling of the Lord is upon your life, whether ministry or layman, take heed and let this young shepherd boy's life be a guide of how we can also be used mightily by the Lord as a shepherd with a true shepherd's heart.

The Lord prepared David to be that shepherd to His people; to feed them, to guide them, to protect them. The integrity of David's heart had truly captured the Lord's attention. That integrity is translated literally as "according to the perfection of his heart". David's heart was so much after God, that it helped him gain favor with the Lord. This scriptural in-sight leads us to search our hearts and say, "Lord, is my heart after you?! Do I have an earnest desire as David had to fulfill all God's will in my life?" Let us ponder these thoughts for a moment as we continue on.

David was no ordinary shepherd boy. David had a heart that was "after God"; this was not common amongst even his own brothers, and the Lord saw that great desire David had to come close to the true

King of Israel – Jehovah. Because of that desire, David was chosen to be king over God's people Israel, God's heritage.

Acts 13:22 says, *"And when he had removed him, he raised up unto them David to be their king; to whom also he gave testimony, and said, I have found David the son of Jesse, <u>a man after mine own heart</u>, which shall fulfil all my will."*

What a glorious testimony was given by the Lord concerning David. This teaches us that he wasn't just another shepherd boy, but he was a man whom the Lord was preparing for great and mighty things. Friend, you too can be made ready for great things. This call of God upon your life isn't to be taken lightly, and if you take your place in the kingdom of God, the Lord will help you to fulfill the ministry the Lord has prepared for you. You may be in your preparation time for His service, or you may be a veteran in the army of the Lord that has carried on the great work of a shepherd of the sheep for many years. But whatever place you are in now, just know the Lord has great things ahead for us all, if we'll just hold on and be faithful. God rewarded David's faithfulness, though he was just a young ruddy boy, and he will reward your faithfulness to Him.

David the shepherd boy knew the dangers of the wilderness by experience. The task given to him by his father Jesse was to guard and protect the flock as he was appointed. Responsibility came early to this Israelite boy, as he was broken from his childhood ways into manhood at an early age. Learning the ways of the wilderness, David learned the tending of the sheep, the concern and care for each and every sheep: it was not a task that could be handled by just anyone. It was a heart-felt occupation that could only be filled by one that truly had the heart of a shepherd. Jesus spoke of this in John 10:12: ***"But he that is an hireling, and not the shepherd, whose own the sheep are not, seeth the wolf coming, and leaveth the sheep, and fleeth: and the wolf catcheth them, and scattereth the sheep."***

God was looking for a shepherd, not a hireling. When the Lord looked at David, he saw something he didn't see in any other young man: he saw the shepherd's heart. He could see the care and compassion he showed to each one of his flock, regardless of the physical condition of that sheep. His heart was being prepared and molded by the Master Shepherd. David, having countless hours to spend in prayer under the heavens, in the solitude of the wilderness, came into close relationship with his heavenly Father. No doubt Jesse had taught his sons about the importance of a reverent fear and love for the God of Israel; of which David did not take lightly. Maybe, as we can imagine, these were the precious times that the Lord was beginning to prepare him for things to come.

Even as our prayer life in this Christian walk so important, to gain the spiritual strength that can only come from the Lord. It helps us to increase our understanding and wisdom in the Word of God, and his precious Holy Ghost. An example can be taken from David's life to use our time wisely; though busy with the cares of life, take special time to spend with our heavenly Father, and it will gain us great fellowship and communion with the Holy Ghost. Could it have been at these times that David's heart began to sing those beautiful Psalms unto the Lord, that we many times overlook because of their regularity in our church services? Could it be that he would sing these hymns in a precious close time with the Lord, with no one to interfere, no one to disturb, no one to get his attention on something else? As we take for example Psalm 23: *"The LORD is my shepherd; I shall not want. He maketh me to lie down in green pastures: he leadeth me beside the still waters. He restoreth my soul: he leadeth me in the paths of righteousness for his name's sake. Yea, though I walk through the valley of the shadow of death, I will fear no evil: for thou art with me; thy rod and thy staff they comfort me. Thou preparest a table before me in the presence of mine enemies: thou anointest my head with oil; my cup runneth over. Surely goodness and mercy shall follow me all the days of my life: and I will dwell in the house of the LORD for ever."*

Oh, what an example this can be for us who know the calling of God upon our lives, and yet don't take advantage of the time to share our thoughts, our praise, our prayers with the Lord that has saved us! Take time for Jesus! He has called us, chosen us, and brought us out of a world of sin. We have much to thank and praise Him for, and He still inhabits the praise of His people, and loves to hear the cries of our hearts! Reach out to Him, for He is so near, even as he was to David! Prayer and time in the presence of the Lord is so critical in the life of a child of God. We certainly won't find the power to overcome this adversary we are talking about without a prayer life that becomes the center of our Christian walk. A writer once said, "Is prayer your steering wheel? Or is it your spare tire?" We can see by this young shepherds' example that having a heart after God meant taking time to call upon the Lord. Another writer said, "A prayer-less soul is a Christ-less soul!" What a powerful statement. We need the communion and fellowship with our heavenly Father that only comes through a devoted prayer life, to gain the power and spiritual strength to escape the wiles of the devil.

Those precious times that David spent in the presence of the Lord prepared him for the battles he was about to face. It made him ready as a strong soldier of the Lord. It prepared his heart to be strong, yet tender to the spirit of God, and obedient to the Lord's every command. Even so will our prayer life prepare us when we make it a priority and not just a habit or religious ritual. It becomes more than just repetition, it becomes life to us. To live, walk, and talk with the Lord on a daily basis is the foundation of a true shepherd, a true servant of the Lord. It is the strength that keeps us when the discouragements of life can overwhelm our souls. We can consider another place in the psalms where David expressed his great need of the Lord's help:

"From the end of the earth will I cry unto thee, when my heart is overwhelmed: lead me to the rock that is higher than I!" (Psalm 61:2)

And he shows his confidence in the Lord's refuge by saying, *"For thou hast been a shelter for me, and a strong tower from the enemy."(v.3)*

Knowing that His God could deliver him from any enemy that would face him, his faith began to grow as he increased in spiritual strength. His desire for the Lord's direction and guidance was shown through the words he wrote and sang unto the Lord.

"The Lord is my light and my salvation; whom shall I fear? The Lord is the strength of my life, of whom shall I be afraid?" (Psalm 27:1)

For us to know the great strength of the God we serve, and not allow Him to lead and guide the steps of our life, it is to our own loss. David wanted to take full advantage of the blessings of the God of Israel, and find a special place in the Lord's kingdom. And that he certainly did. The Lord shaped and molded this young shepherd into the man of God he needed to be, preparing him for great things and the throne of Israel.

A very special day came in the life of David when the prophet Samuel came to Bethlehem unexpectedly. Samuel had been sent by the Lord to the house of Jesse, to find a new king amongst his sons. The Lord had spoken to Samuel after He rejected Saul from being king because of Saul's presumptive disobedience.

Disobedience to God will cost you everything!
Saul learned that the hard way. The scripture says, *"And the LORD said unto Samuel, How long wilt thou mourn for Saul, seeing I have rejected him from reigning over Israel? fill thine horn with oil, and go, I will send thee to Jesse the Bethlehemite: for I have provided me a king among his sons."(1Samuel 16:1)*
Samuel had not shared the heavenly vision with anyone, and his visit to the town was a great surprise to many. Even the elders of the town were shaken at his presence. Samuel announced his purpose that he had come to sacrifice to the Lord and called Jesse and his sons to sanctify their selves, and come to the sacrifice.

As Samuel looked upon the sons of Jesse, he earnestly believed that God had chosen of the strongest and eldest of them. But to Samuel's amazement, the Lord refused them. As Samuel looked upon Jesse's eldest son, the Lord spoke to Samuel as the scripture says; *"But the LORD said unto Samuel, Look not on his countenance, or on the height of his stature; because I have refused him: for the LORD seeth not as man seeth; for man looketh on the outward appearance, but the LORD looketh on the heart.(1 Samuel 16:7)*

What we see with our natural eye is not what the Lord sees. He was searching for a heart; a heart that would be true to Him: a heart that would love and obey His every command. He was looking for a heart that was after Him! Not seeking the position, not the fame or fortune, but seeking after the Lord!

At this point, we can take this example and we can learn what the Lord is searching for in us. He looks and searches the hearts of his people, his ministers, for one that will love and obey him regardless of the consequences. Our precious Jesus, our Savior, is looking to those that will love him, and have a true heart after HIM! Not the fame, popularity, the position; but leaving off every fleshly ambition, to find that precious relationship with the King of Kings and Lord of Lords! Have we as his people, His shepherds, pointed our hearts in his direction? Have we committed our ways to his instruction, allowing Him to be everything to us? Are we to only be a person seeking a position in the church or the pulpit?

Are we looking unto Him for every step we take, every move we make? Are we allowing His Holy Ghost to lead and guide us into all his truth, and declaring His infallible Gospel with all of our hearts?! Young person, have you totally surrendered to the Lord's will for your life? Or are you seeking your own ambitions, in a world of immoral corruption that can only destroy your eternal soul? Total surrender is what He expects from each and every one of us. As David, an innocent young ruddy shepherd boy had his heart after the great God of Israel, so must we have our hearts clean from sin, and purely devoted to seek Him, love Him, and obey Him! Let these thoughts provoke us to seek the Lord as never before, and allow Him to make us a man or woman after God's heart!

Every one of Jesse's sons passed before Samuel the prophet, and every one the Lord rejected. Samuel asked Jesse if this were all his sons, and Jesse replied, *"There remaineth yet the youngest, and, behold, he keepeth the sheep. And Samuel said unto Jesse, Send and fetch him: for we will not sit down till he come hither. And he sent, and brought him in. Now he was ruddy, and withal of a beautiful countenance, and goodly to look to. And the LORD said, Arise, anoint him: for this is he. Then Samuel took the horn of oil, and anointed him in the midst of his brethren: and the Spirit of the LORD came upon David from that day forward. (v.11-13)*

This was the greatest day of David's life in the Lord! What a miracle, that the Lord would choose a young ruddy shepherd boy; to anoint him to the next king of Israel?! We can't imagine the power and blessing he felt as that glorious horn of anointing oil was poured upon his head by Samuel. As it was poured upon Him, what an amazing change that came over his life! That same anointing of the Holy Ghost belongs to those who will have a heart after God! When Samuel anointed David in the midst of his brethren, the spirit of the Lord came upon him from that day forward. And even so we can receive that glorious anointing of the Holy Ghost in our lives, and be filled with His spirit and power! This is how the grace of God works in the lives of those who will look to him and trust Him for His every promise, and fulfillment of His living Word! To you these promises belong, if we will believe and stand upon them, allowing our hearts to be after our Lord Jesus! Even so the promise of an anointing to come upon us has been given. Jesus said, *"But ye shall receive power after that the Holy Ghost is come upon you." (Acts 1:8)*

This is the Lord's promise to everyone that repents and is baptized: the Holy Ghost will come upon your life and anoint you to the work of the Lord. This great gift of God is still working in the church today, we must ask Him to anoint us! This is what we live and strive for; to be filled with a heart after Jesus, He will anoint us to the promises and will of God, and bring us true victory over the enemy. There is no other way to overcome this ugly lion that roars against us, except through the power of the Holy Ghost. The glorious third person of the trinity was sent to us on the day of Pentecost to anoint and prepare a people to do great things for the kingdom of God. Unfortunately, sin has crept into the modern church today, and we have left aside the true anointing of the Holy Ghost that sanctifies and creates a clean heart and a clean life within the child of God. But the same spirit of God that met David that day is the same Holy Ghost power that can come upon a life that is seeking after the Lord. Now David was prepared to meet any enemy he might face, any trial that would come his way. It wasn't going to be an easy road, but the Lord being his help and his anointing, he would have the victory.

We don't know every fact about David's experiences as a shepherd in his young life, but we can gain some insight by reading his writings, and some of the writings in the book of first Samuel. As he guarded the flock with all care, the wilderness held many unseen dangers. There was an enemy that lurked about, seeking to devour this young shepherd boy and his flock. David had some knowledge of the dangers of the wilderness, and he had encountered some obstacles as well in caring for the flock. But when the enemy came up against him to destroy, he had to learn and depend upon a hand that would fight for him, mightier than David could imagine. It was the hand of the Lord!

We are now coming to the point in David's life where this anointing from God was going to be put to the test. This is the part of David's life that taught him how to overcome when the enemy came against him. As David guarded the sheep, a lion and a bear came and stole a sheep from the flock. Does this sound familiar? Pastors, when the enemy comes in disguised, in sheep's clothing, and with subtlety steals away with one of the Lord's sheep, it is heartbreaking. When we know the intents of the devil, and we see his wiles working against the congregation, to steal, kill, and destroy, something begins to rise up within us and tell us to fight for that one sheep! The Holy Ghost says fight! Believe the Lord for the victory over Satan that has their eyes blinded, and in faith take back those lost sheep. David, in godly vengeance, and in his love for the sheep, pursued after those wild beasts to take back what had been stolen. We are not given all the details of this event in the scriptures, but we are given to know that through the power and spirit of the Lord, David overcame those wild beasts, and slew them to rescue his lost sheep. Surely that lion and bear roared against him; so David by faith put his life in the hands of the Lord, and slew that terrible roaring lion and bear with his own hands! Once again **GOD SHUT THE LION'S MOUTH!!** What a mighty

God we serve! As we are commissioned to bring in the lost sheep to the Lord, there are many times the devil will roar and rage to tear a sheep away from us and our flock (the church). He rages to bring into captivity every soul that he can. But through the blood of Jesus and the anointing of the Holy Ghost, the Lord can shut the lion's mouth, defeat the enemy, and put him to flight. Jesus knows how to give his people victory over the enemy! And through the great power and authority that is given to us to defeat our enemy, no matter how strong, we will win the battle, and are made more than conquerors and victors through Jesus!

Jesus said, *"Behold I give you power to tread on serpents and scorpions, and over all the power of the enemy: and nothing shall by any means hurt you." (Luke 10:19)* This is God's promise to us if we believe and serve Him, and allow him to anoint us with the Holy Ghost, He will fight every battle for us and give us power over any enemy that roars against us!

This situation gave David the courage to once again stand against an enemy to rescue the sheep of Israel. David, being sent by Jesse his father to visit his brethren in the midst of battle with the Philistines, heard and witnessed another terrible enemy: a giant Philistine named Goliath, as he came and blasphemed the God of Israel and His armies. We can imagine how that valley rang as this enemy roared as a lion against the armies of Israel, and challenged them to a battle. But once again, the anointing in David's life from the Lord raised up in a godly vengeance, as the cursing and blaspheming of this giant pierced his soul and mind. Immediately, faith and power came alive in his soul, and he declared his holy manifesto to King Saul that he would go and face the enemy that was challenging the armies of the Lord. He rehearsed the story of God's deliverance from the paw of the lion and the bear before the king, and let him know that he had the courage to go face that roaring enemy, Goliath. Fear and doubt were put aside, and the anointing of the Lord began to take over in this young man's heart, that heart that was certainly after God!

There are times when the challenges of life come up against us as a giant, too big to overcome. Especially to you who are called into the ministry. The enemy loves to attack the head, reach for the top, and do all he can to get us to surrender to the pressures of every evil device he can throw at us. Why is it that every year so many pastors resign their churches? Why is it that so many ministers are leaving the ministry to pursue other secular careers? How can it be that many shepherds are letting down the banner of the blood of Jesus and His Gospel, and taking up with doctrines that will mislead and destroy the flock? Could it be that the roar of that enemy has shaken the foundations of faith in the lives of many that at one time were used to carry the Gospel, spread the good news, and lead the dying into the glorious light of life?

We refer back to our scripture at the beginning of chapter one: ***Be sober, be vigilant; because your adversary the devil, <u>as a roaring lion</u>, walketh about, seeking whom he may devour: (1 Peter 5:8)***

We have underlined those words "as a roaring lion". Those words being translated in the Greek as "in that manner": it tells us that his roar may seem to be great and mighty, but is truly not mighty or great. He is denoting the efforts which he makes to alarm and overpower us. The lion here is not the crouching lion - the lion stealth fully creeping toward his foe. But it is the raging monarch of the woods, who by his terrible roar would *intimidate* all so that they might become an easy prey. Certainly this is what the devil is good at: **intimidation**! He uses it against us all, especially towards the shepherd who is enduring persecution, ridicule, sometimes even slander and criticism. He would like to discourage the ministry to the point of intimidation, where we are no longer the anointed spiritual shepherds of the flock, but weak, feeble, unfaithful people who don't care to face the enemy and fight. We cannot give in, and we certainly can't give up! Who will carry the message if we allow this lying enemy, who uses tactics that could easily deceive the weak into falling prey to his teeth, and bring us to a place of surrender to his wicked desires? We cannot allow the enemy to win over us. We must do as David, and take up our manifesto that we will not bow nor surrender to the enemy!

The psalmist we are reading and talking about today was many times faced with these feelings of intimidation; feelings of persecution and betrayal, even by those whom he led and protected by his own hands.

Psalm 118:13 says, *"Thou hast thrust sore at me that I might fall: but the LORD helped me."* And again he says in Psalm 18:17, *"He delivered me from my strong enemy, and from them which hated me: for they were too strong for me.*

There was no lack of those fierce enemies that roared the roar of intimidation against David; but he knew where to find his strength. His strength came from the Lord. Another Psalm that he wrote says, *"I will lift up mine eyes unto the hills, from when cometh my help. My help cometh from the Lord which made heaven and earth." (Psalm 121:1-2)*
We must look to the Lord when these feelings of intimidation, fear, doubt, and unbelief try to overtake us. Many are giving in to a spirit of fear in these last days, but we cannot surrender to the pressures of this life. We must hold onto the faith we have received

and run with the anointing of the Lord working in our lives. If you lack what you need, seek the Lord, turn to Him, and allow Him to strengthen, anoint and encourage you. Our help comes from the Lord!

The blasphemous Philistine giant came up again to challenge the armies of Israel, and David once again heard his cursing. Let us read the account in the scriptures:

"And David said to Saul, Let no man's heart fail because of him; thy servant will go and fight with this Philistine. And Saul said to David, Thou art not able to go against this Philistine to fight with him: for thou art but a youth, and he a man of war from his youth. And David said unto Saul, Thy servant kept his father's sheep, and there came a lion, and a bear, and took a lamb out of the flock: And I went out after him, and smote him, and delivered it out of his mouth: and when he arose against me, I caught him by his beard, and smote him, and slew him. Thy servant slew both the lion and the bear: and this uncircumcised Philistine shall be as one of them, seeing he hath defied the armies of the living God. David said moreover, The LORD that delivered me out of the paw of the lion, and out of the paw of the bear, he will deliver me out of the hand of this Philistine. And Saul said unto David, Go, and the LORD be with thee. (1 Samuel 17:32-37)

This was not just an act of courage and bravery, nor of a skilled soldier trained to face the enemy on the front line: this was a shepherd boy, who in the face of the enemy, didn't lean upon his own understanding: he trusted in the Lord. This giant Philistine named Goliath was more than just an enemy; he was the dividing obstacle between victory and defeat for the Israelites. The great God of Israel would give the army of Israel victory over any enemy, but fear and doubt became as big an obstacle as the giant that was challenging them.

Are there giants in your life that are challenging you? They appear taller, stronger, and more powerful than we are. Have you found yourself questioning whether the Lord can deliver you out of the mouth of the lion? Has unbelief become so great an obstacle, that you haven't been able to experience the Lord's great deliverance in your life over sin, sickness, infirmity, plagues, habits, and addictions? The sad truth is that many in the church, and sometimes in the pulpit, have become slaves to a giant, that is truly not a giant, but a messenger of Satan, sent by the devil to roar and intimidate, and cause us to doubt and disbelieve that Jesus can set us free.

We must look at the things that are robbing us of our faith and overcome these obstacles. The influence of Hollywood, social media, the internet, secular outlets, etc., have claimed their place in the lives of many Christians. These things have become an addictive giant that is destroying many souls. Satan has even claimed his seat in many homes and in many churches. If we are not careful, we put ourselves in that lion's roaring mouth, opening ourselves up to demonic influence, and become prey to every device of the devil. His tactics and his wiles are deceitful and destructive, if we allow ourselves to fall prey to his devices. But committing ourselves to God, and believing His mighty promises will always outweigh anything that this enemy can throw at us.

James tells us in his writings, ***"Submit yourselves therefore to God. Resist the devil and he will flee from you." (James 4:7)*** Our submission to God and His will is the secret to having victory over the devil and his devices. When I submit myself to God's will, the devil has to flee, because then my Heavenly Father sends the Holy Ghost to fight my battle and give me victory! There is no way the devil can stay when the blood of Jesus has washed my soul, cleansed and delivered me, and given me the Holy Ghost to sanctify me, and keep me from all evil. We are victors every time when we do it the Lord's way.

This is what David learned: if he would submit to the Lord's will, allow the anointing and spirit of God upon his life to take control, there was no enemy that could stand against him. We have the same opportunity to see the devil flee from us, and even more so because we have the blood of Jesus, and our great Shepherd of the sheep fighting for us! Nothing shall by any means harm us if we obey the word of the Lord and we shall see the devil cast out!

Now David was ready. Saul offered his armor to David, but David refused knowing he hadn't proved himself worthy to wear that armor. We can see also that David realized this battle was not his, it belonged to God. Today friend, dear brother and sister, that battle is not yours; it belongs to the Lord. Let Him fight this battle for you! David didn't look for earthly weapons or armor, knowing the anointing given to him would gain him the advantage over any enemy he would face. So it is with the child of God. When the Lord anoints us, he prepares and equips us for the battle. We must strive to prepare ourselves as Jesus taught; watching, fasting, and praying. We must allow the Word of God to fill our souls with the strength and faith to believe the Lord, no matter how big the giant seems to be.

The scripture says that David *"took his staff in his hand, and chose him five smooth stones out of the brook, and put them in a shepherd's bag which he had, even in a scrip; and his sling was in his hand: and he drew near to the Philistine.(1 Samuel 17:40)*

David now took to the offensive: he was going to face that giant regardless of the consequences, because he knew that His God was fighting for him. With the simplest of weapons in his hand, he put his trust in the Lord, not in the sword or spear. Even as we must know that this battle is a spiritual battle, not a physical battle. Satan as a lion, as a giant, roars against us thinking he has the victory over us. But as

David, we must declare our manifesto that God is our refuge and deliverer. As he told Saul, *"The **LORD** that delivered me out of the paw of the lion, and out of the paw of the bear, he will deliver me out of the hand of this Philistine."* By faith he spoke that God would deliver him, and not allow the enemy that was roaring against the children of God to destroy Him. There are times we must look back through our past life in the Lord, and remember the many testimonies of deliverance and miracles that He has given to us. Not to mention His many great promises given to us in His Word, and He isn't finished with his church yet! The great and mighty Lamb of God that taketh away the sins of the world is that mighty King of Kings and Lord of Lords that comes to do battle for us! That should make us shout the victory when we think of what Jesus has done for us! Can you just give Him the praise, for all He has done in your life! David remembered that the Lord had brought him through before and he would do it again! For all He's done, we will lift our hands and praise Him! For all He's done, we will live our lives to please Him!

As David approached the giant, Goliath cursed David by his gods, and disdained him, realizing he was but a ruddy youth. But he wasn't aware of the power that was working through the anointing in this young man's life. The invisible weapons of the Spirit of the Lord were going to wage war against a physical, ungodly giant that had blasphemed the God of Israel. This would put an end to the threat of a giant that had roared against them for the last time. David made his declaration, his manifesto to this giant, that he would have the victory over him because of the Lord.

The scripture says, *"Then said David to the Philistine, Thou comest to me with a sword, and with a spear, and with a shield: but I come to thee in the name of the LORD of hosts, the God of the armies of Israel, whom thou hast defied. This day will the LORD deliver thee into mine hand; and I will smite thee, and take thine head from thee; and I will give the carcases of the host of the Philistines this day unto the fowls of the air, and to the wild beasts of the earth; that all the earth may know that there is a God in Israel. And all this assembly shall know that the LORD saveth not with sword and spear: for the battle is the LORD'S, and he will give you into our hands." (1 Samuel 17:45-47)*

Now the fight was on, and the challenge had been met by a challenger sent by God. David was God's representative, sent to bring deliverance to the nation of Israel. And as the Lord shows by his power, it would not be by the physical ability or might of the natural man, but by demonstration of the spirit and power of God. David knew that battle was too great for him, but it wasn't too great for his God. He looked at that looming giant, as he roared threats of death against him; but still with faith burning in his heart, he reached into his shepherd's bag, took a stone and put it in his sling. He began to swing in the name of the Lord, in the power and might of the spirit of God, until that small smooth stone launched from his sling and smote the giant in the most vulnerable place: his forehead! What a mighty God we serve, the greatest General and Captain of the Host of the armies of the Lord, who fights our every battle! With immeasurable force that stone pierced the giant's weakest point and brought him down to the ground in defeat! The battle was over! We must trust the Lord in the same way to believe that He will fight our battles, even now as the lion roars against us to destroy us. No matter how fierce, how powerful he may seem, he still has no power over our God! How great is our GOD!

What a great example is given to us in this simple Bible story that we have read since we were children in Sunday school. To apply this passage to our lives today is needful, as the adversary is pursuing, threatening, intimidating, and discouraging so many of God's people. Our faith has become small to these giants, and instead of being victors, we have cowardly withdrawn into the background, even as the armies of Israel did, hoping that this wicked enemy would just go away. But he must be cast out! He must be faced head on with the faith and power that comes through the anointing of the Holy Ghost! Pastors, shepherds of the flock: we must take up our banners, uphold our standards: **PREACH THE WORD! DECLARE THE VICTORY!** Face the enemy in the spirit and power of the Holy Ghost, believing that Jesus can still cast out the devil that is trying to influence our lives, our churches, and our families by his intimidating roar of doubt and fear! We are not going to escape the temptation and trying of our faith in this life; it is sure that we will have to go through. But the scripture says, "*For I reckon that the sufferings of this present time are not worthy to be compared with the glory which shall be revealed in us." (Romans 8:18)* There is great glory ahead to those that will hold on to the end to gain that glorious crown of life the Lord has prepared for them that love Him.

To assure the victory, David ran to the giant, pulled out the giant's own sword, and slew him, and cut off his head. Victory was won, because a young shepherd boy trusted God to **SHUT THE LIONS MOUTH!** What David did was make sure the enemy was dead and no longer a threat. We can't escape the threat of the devil in this life, because he is constantly roaring against the church and God's people. But we can declare him a defeated foe, and through the blood of Jesus and the power of the Holy Ghost have victory over his wicked devices. We can take authority over the sins and habits that would so easily beset us, cut that giants head off in our lives: unbelief, fear, doubt, worry, even sin and addiction. Take the Word of God as our weapon, and we can gain the victory over him. And in the end we will see him defeated and destroyed for eternity in the lake of fire by the King of Kings and Lord of Lords. What a day of rejoicing that will be!

Now, it is our time to trust the Lord, knowing that Jesus is still the Author and finisher or our faith; Take the sword of the spirit and cut off the enemy's ugly head, declaring him defeated, and that our God is still God in all! Though the enemy roars at us with terrible vengeance, we must know that Jesus is fighting the battle for us, and will bring us to the place of TOTAL VICTORY!

"For by thee I have run through a troop; and by my God have I leaped over a wall. As for God, his way is perfect: the word of the LORD is tried: he is a buckler to all those that trust in him. For who is God save the LORD? or who is a rock save our God? It is God that girdeth me with strength, and maketh my way perfect. He maketh my feet like hinds' feet, and setteth me upon my high places. He teacheth my hands to war, so that a bow of steel is broken by mine arms. Thou hast also given me the shield of thy salvation: and thy right hand hath holden me up, and thy gentleness hath made me great. Thou hast enlarged my steps under me, that my feet did not slip. I have pursued mine enemies, and overtaken them: neither did I turn again till they were consumed. I have wounded them that they were not able to rise: they are fallen under my feet. For thou hast girded me with strength unto the battle: thou hast subdued under me those that rose up against me."   *(Psalm 18:29-39)*

CHAPTER THREE:

SAMSON – THE MAN OF GREAT STRENGTH

"And the Spirit of the LORD began to move him at times in the camp of Dan" (Judges 13:25)

In the previous chapters we have discussed the characters and acts of two men of great spiritual faith and strength in the Lord. Two great examples given to us in the Word of God to teach us that we can have power over the enemy that roars and fights against us in the spirit. This is what the Lord plans for His children; for us to be the overcomer, the victor, through His blood and by His spirit.

Now we will look at the life of a man who was given great strength physically to judge the nation of Israel, and bring them deliverance from the captivity of the Philistines. His name was Samson. We will study his life, and very important parts of his life that can help us as we strive to be the Lord's overcomers.

Samson was born to Manoah and his wife, of the tribe of Dan, and prepared as a Nazarite from his mother's womb. This was to be no ordinary child or son. The call of the Lord was upon his life, and he was purposed to do great things for the kingdom of God. The commandment of the Lord concerning the Nazarites was a very special high calling, devoting the life of the person to the Lord through a special vow. This vow was sacred, holy, and not to be taken lightly. It was a lifelong vow, and in the case of Samson, as the angel commanded his parents to dedicate him as a Nazarite even from birth, as a perfectly dedicated life to the Lord, undefiled and separate from sin. *(You can find the commandment of the Nazarites in Numbers 6:1-21)*

When we think of our lives as children of God, or even those that are called to ministry for His kingdom, our vow to that call and commitment to the Lord must be taken very seriously. The scriptures tell us that we must be dedicated, consecrated, and committed to the Lord with all of our hearts. Romans 12:1-2 says, *"I beseech you therefore, brethren, by the mercies of God, that ye present your bodies a living sacrifice, holy, acceptable unto God, **which is** your reasonable service. And be not conformed to this world: but be ye transformed by the renewing of your mind, that ye may prove what **is** that good, and acceptable, and perfect, will of God."*

Presenting ourselves to the Lord by being a living sacrifice unto him, dedicated and committed to His holy purpose for our lives is what He desires from each of His children. The ministry is a sacred position, taking a sacred post behind a sacred desk, and only those who are truly committed to the Lord, holy unto Him, can fulfill such a calling. The honor of bearing the sword of the spirit, the Word of God, is the highest calling that can be given to a man. Even so was the vow and calling of the Nazarite. It was a command to not be "conformed to this world, but transformed!" This is the calling of every child of God that is saved, to be dedicated, committed, and holy unto the Lord!

An angel sent from the Lord brought the message to Manoah's wife because she had been barren and not able to conceive. He promised her a son from the Lord: but he also warned her to take heed to keep from anything that would defile the calling on her child's life.

The scripture says, *"And the angel of the LORD appeared unto the woman, and said unto her, Behold now, thou art barren, and bearest not: but thou shalt conceive, and bear a son. Now therefore beware, I pray thee, and drink not wine nor strong drink, and eat not any unclean thing: For, lo, thou shalt conceive, and bear a son; and no razor shall come on his head: for the child shall be a Nazarite unto God from the womb: and he shall begin to deliver Israel out of the hand of the Philistines. (Judges 13:3-5)*

It was critical for Manoah's wife to keep herself clean from defilement, while she carried this child promised from the Lord. This is a great example for the parents of today: your child is looking to you for the example. How you live, act, walk, talk, will be the example your child will follow after. Many parents don't realize what an influence they have on their children. Even as expectant parents, prayer and much care should be given for direction and guidance in your new child's life. This is an eternal soul placed in your responsibility by the Lord. A soul that one day will give an account for all his deeds and acts. So there is a great responsibility laid upon parents to lead and guide your children in the way of the Lord. Even from birth you are molding and shaping their character, as the Lord begins to deal with their hearts. You are the image they see in this life, and until they reach the age to come to know the Lord, you are the example they will follow. Be that example to your children the Lord has called you to be, and see your child grow into a great man or woman of God.

This woman could have despised the commandment of the angel, and Samson would not have received the blessing and dedication of being that Nazarite the Lord was calling him to be. We must be responsible examples to our children and others alike, so that they can also follow in the footsteps of Jesus: Taking on the whole armor of God, to withstand the wiles of the devil, and the fierce roars of the enemy.

The angel once again appeared to Manoah and his wife the second time, and confirmed the promise again. We know when the Lord makes a promise he confirms it in the mouth of two or three witnesses. That enforces the surety of His promise. Manoah and his wife believed the angel of the Lord, and did as the Lord had instructed them, to keep their child in the ways of the Lord, strictly abiding by the commandments of the Lord concerning the Nazarite vow.

This leads us to a very important thought concerning this young child born to Manoah and his wife. He was not only going to be dedicated to the will of God for his life, but he also was going to be used as a mighty warrior to judge and deliver his people out of the hands of the enemy, the Philistines. This is a great example to us, as the Lord's servants. The calling of the Lord upon your life is so important, child of God and servant of the Lord, because it is not only the deliverance of our own spiritual souls, but also to reach the many lost and dying that Satan has in his clenches. This calling is a holy and high calling; to be called as the children of the most High God. But He is looking for soul winners that will be dedicated to His will, and hungry to reach the lost at any cost, as Jude says: *"And of some have compassion, making a difference: And others save with fear, pulling them out of the fire; hating even the garment spotted by the flesh. (Jude 1:22-23)*

Souls are perishing, and the Lord is looking for a Nazarite he can trust to carry the Gospel to them before it is too late. Ask yourself today, "Am I doing all that I can to reach my family, my children, the lost?" Ponder that thought for a moment.

Manoah's wife gave birth to a son, and they called his name Samson. The scripture says, *"And the woman bare a son, and called his name Samson: and the child grew, and the LORD blessed him. And the Spirit of the LORD began to move him at times in the camp of Dan between Zorah and Eshtaol. (Judges 13:24-25)*

Because of the dedication of Samson to the Lord, the Lord blessed him in his youth, and the Spirit of the Lord began to work in his life at a young age. This should be a great encouragement to parents that are raising their children in the ways of the Lord, and to young people who are seeking to find their place in the service of the Lord. Young person, the Lord can use your life if you make yourself available. We are living in a day when our younger generation has been captivated by Satan's luring temptations of sin, worldly amusements, lust, drugs, social media, and the internet outlets that lead to a number of destructive devices for our youth. Even the public school system and college education system have become a training ground for the devil to destroy the lives of our young people. It is very important for us as ministers of the Lord to encourage our youth in godliness, holy living, and commitment to the things of God, instead of entertainment, the self-appetites of the flesh, and the humanistic teachings in the public schools. This is such a great example, especially to parents, that if we will lead, our children will follow in the paths of righteousness. We must be the example. The Holy Ghost can use a vessel that is dedicated, consecrated, and prepared for the Master's use. As Samson had to learn, this life was and is full of the devil's roars of temptation that steal the very spirit and faith in God out of your heart if we allow it. As the spirit of the Lord began to move in his life, so the roars of temptation began to come against him also.

Samson had a fault that would later prove to be his ruin. He found himself looking and desiring the

Philistine women. This is why we must always consider the examples in scripture given to us, and apply to our lives only those that lead us to righteousness. Samson's life was not always one that we would follow, as to please the Lord: he was designed not to be a pattern to us (we must walk by rule, not by example). We are to walk by God's law and rule, not according to man's thoughts or ways, or even their example. We must keep our eyes on the Author and Finisher of our faith, Jesus!

One Philistine woman in particular caught his eye, and he told his parents he wanted this daughter of the Philistines for his wife. But his parents were greatly saddened by the desire of their son that was dedicated to the Lord. This is a subject we will expound more in depth later in the chapter, as we find how Satan uses these devices to destroy the righteous, and how seemingly small sins if allowed to continue are the beginning of greater sins.

Samson's parents, though against this union, gave in and took Samson to meet the woman. Little did they know that the Lord was going to allow this to be used as an occasion to gain victory over the Philistine army. The Lord has a plan in all things.

As they made their journey to Timnath to meet the Philistine woman, Samson must have taken a separate path through the vineyards of Timnath alone, which led him into an encounter that unexpectedly challenged his strength and faith. These are the types of encounters that come against us to challenge our faith and spiritual strength, as the adversary, the devil roars against us to challenge us in spiritual warfare. Could this have come because Samson took a detour instead of staying on the same path with his parents? Certainly the Lord had a plan, but there are times when we get detoured, or sidetracked, and the enemy sets an ambush for us. Only the mercy of the Lord can spare us as it spared Samson that day. Sometimes we don't realize how close to death we walk. The scripture says, *"Then went Samson down, and his father and his mother, to Timnath, and came to the vineyards of Timnath: and, behold, a young lion roared against him. (Judges 14:5)*

This was a death defying challenge: Samson, attacked unexpectedly by a young lion that roared against him, had to find the faith and strength to defend himself against this fierce beast. The strength of a young lion was great, as it would fiercely attack his prey, would not lose his catch, until it had taken life. Samson found himself in the direct contact with the king of the beasts; a beast that was determined to take the life of his prey without mercy. It is to be noticed that the word used here for lion does not mean a whelp, but one that has "attained its strength, and is full of the natural fierceness." This means a terrible lion, one with a bloodthirsty character, or that has all its natural savageness of nature fully developed.

What a great comparison of the spiritual battle you

may be facing today: in this example, it was a fleshly battle, but for us, it is a spiritual battle. A spiritual lion, fierce and bold, unexpectedly roars and attacks you from out of nowhere. The enemy rages in triumph thinking he will cleverly outsmart and defeat you. His plan is to catch you off guard, when you're not praying, not spending time in God's Word, not staying on the straight path toward heaven, but sidetracked or complacent. Then comes the ambush. Satan comes as a roaring lion, and attacks you with a temptation, a bad report, a sickness, trouble with your family, problems in the church; the list goes on and on. In the midst of it all, you find yourself full of doubt and fear because this has caught you unaware.

How careful we must be to always watch and pray. Some of the simplest teachings that Jesus gave his disciples is what will help us to overcome these types of situations. Jesus said, *"The thief cometh not, but for to steal, and to kill, and to destroy: (John 10:10)* He also warned us to *"Watch and pray, that ye enter not into temptation: the spirit indeed is willing, but the flesh is weak. (Matt. 26:41)* The Lord Jesus was well acquainted with the wicked lion that roars against God's people, and knew of the frailties and weakness of the flesh: so he warned his disciples of how to prepare for these attacks. The Psalmist David, as he saw the sufferings of Christ afar off, prophesied of how the Lord would face these things. Psalm 22:13 says, *"They gaped upon me with their mouths, as a ravening and a roaring lion."* The prophets spoke of the suffering of Jesus, and the great enemies that would face him at the cross. That is why we must take heed to follow the instructions of the Master, trust in His guiding hand, and know that He knows how to deliver us out of the mouth of the lion! This enemy comes to steal, to kill, and to destroy: but as Jesus said, *"I am come that they might have life, and that they might have it more abundantly."* (John 10:10) Believe the promises of the Lord and He will bring you through that battle, that trial, and that temptation! HE WILL NOT FAIL YOU! You can count on Jesus! He will send His Holy Ghost to give you power to overcome the temptation set before you.

Even again in the Psalms, David spoke of the vicious adversary that was set to destroy through persecution, both spiritually and physically. Psalms 7:1-2 says, *"O LORD my God, in thee do I put my trust: save me from all them that persecute me, and deliver me: Lest he tear my soul like a lion, rending it in pieces, while there is none to deliver."* As we can see by these prophetic scriptures, the devil has no mercy, but seeks to destroy all whom he can. As our theme in this book tells us, *"he walks about as a roaring lion seeking whom he may devour."* Oh that this warning would keep us always on our guard! These spiritual attacks are unavoidable for the child of God; but we have a great consolation that money cannot buy. We have the God of heaven, and His Son Jesus, with the power of the Holy Ghost and all of heaven on our side, fighting for us. We know that it is not His will that any should perish, but *that all should come to the knowledge of repentance (2 Peter 3:9)* Though He allows Satan to tempt, test, and try our faith and patience, He is faithful to make a way of escape. He gives us power to defeat the enemy and overcome the temptation. Through the power of the blood of Jesus shed upon the cross, and the anointing of His precious Holy Ghost, we have the power! Take advantage of the gifts that the Lord has placed within your life, and allow the Lord to use those gifts to give you victory!

As Samson was attacked by this ferocious enemy, the spirit of the Lord came alive in him, and he defeated the lion. The scripture tells us *"And the Spirit of the LORD came mightily upon him, and he rent him as he would have rent a kid, and he had nothing in his hand:" (Judges 14:6)* The word "rent" in the Hebrew speaks of "splitting or tearing", which means he tore the lion with his bare hands. He had no weapon, no sword, not so much as a knife: but the Spirit of the Lord and the power of God that gave him to strength to do such a mighty act, and delivered him out of the mouth of the lion! Praise God for His amazing wonders!

Today, you can also be given the strength to overcome that lion that is roaring against you. Even when you have an attack of the enemy that comes and is so unexpected, the Lord can give you power over that enemy, as He did to Samson! It pays to serve the Lord, and to be faithful unto Him! To have someone that can fight our every battle, and keep us from all danger and harm! It is more than just luck or good fortune, it's a miracle! The miraculous power of God that can live in a child of God, and helps us to be more than conquerors through Him that loved us! He wants to place that power and anointing in our lives to help us to be an overcomer. Let Jesus fill your vessel to overflowing, so that you can be that example to your family, friends, church brothers and sisters. They too can know the wonder working power in the precious blood of Jesus, and His wonderful Holy Ghost!

Are you facing a spiritual lion right now? Has that roar and rage of his fierceness caused you to doubt or disbelieve the Lord can deliver you? These are real situations that people faced in the Bible, and as they overcame, we too can overcome by the blood of Jesus, and by the Holy Ghost. There is nothing impossible with God. Submission, obedience, and faith will make all the difference. Through Samson's dedication to the Lord as a Nazarite, the Lord was able to give him superhuman strength to defeat this ferocious beast. This is why our consecration and dedication to the Lord is so important. It keeps us from sin, and builds our spiritual strength to help us fight the good fight of faith, and hold on to the Lord's truth. That is why Paul the apostle wrote to the church at Ephesus, and told them, *"Be strong in the Lord and in the power of His might. Put on the whole armour of God that ye may be able to stand against the wiles of the devil." (Ephesians 6:11-12)* Our spiritual strength only comes from the Lord, and through our seeking this strength from the Lord, He will give us the power to overcome.

There is a great spirit of deception plaguing the religious world today, not to mention the secular world as well. Everywhere we turn there is a great roaring lion of deception, lying and deceiving if any way possible, to deceive even God's elect. Our warning came from the Lord Jesus himself as he told his disciples, *"Take heed that no man deceive you." (Matthew 24:4)* This was one of the first signs that Jesus told us to look for in the last days. And we are here! Deception is all around us! From the government to the media, political agendas and today's educational systems, it can be seen in all areas. When we realize that it is destroying lives, and devouring the countless souls of young and old, it brings sorrow to the godly heart and a burden for us to help spread the truth. We must stand up in spiritual strength, take the offensive to fight the devil, and on the defensive, protect the truth of God's word that others might be saved. We can be used by the Lord to shut the lion's mouth!

We are living in the day when all these things shall be fulfilled as we approach the soon coming of our Lord. So we must be ready. Jesus said, *"Blessed are those servants, whom the lord when he cometh shall find watching:" (Luke 12:37) "Be ye therefore ready also: for the Son of man cometh at an hour when ye think not." (v.40)*

Jesus forewarned and told us of these days, and we need to take heed to the warnings that we not be deceived or led astray from God's truth. Remember, the truth shall make you free! Free from the lies and the roars of a deceitful enemy that wants to plague us with fear. But remember that God's perfect love casts out all fear, and gives us that perfect peace we need in our lives. The peace that passes all understanding, and the faith to know that God will deliver us! God proves his love and faithfulness to us in the times of the most difficult and overwhelming battles and trials in our lives. Things we could not overcome naturally, the Lord uses to help us to realize we must lean upon him in full dependency.

As Samson returned to the land of the Philistines, he once again came to the carcass of the lion he battled. Inside the carcass of the lion was a swarm of bees and honey. This is a perfect picture of how the Lord gives us complete deliverance, and brings us sweetness, even in bitter times. When the enemy is raging against you, Jesus can speak peace to that storm and give you the sweetness of His spirit, the strength of His Holy Ghost, and the touch of His mighty hand. We have all of heaven fighting in our favor to bring us to victory, and know that we still have the victory in Jesus!

Samson had many other acts of heroic faith and supernatural strength given to him by the Lord. He slew many of the Philistines to bring the children of God deliverance from their oppressors. Another great deliverance the Lord gave to Samson happened in Lehi, when the Philistines came to take Samson captive. As the enemy shouted against him *(the lion's roar)*, the Spirit of the Lord came mightily upon him, and the cords he was bound with became as **"flax that was burnt with fire, and his bands loosed from off his hands." (Judges 15:14)** In that moment, the Lord helped him find the jawbone of a donkey, by which he slew a thousand men. Victory came that day as he allowed the Spirit of the Lord to use his life to grant deliverance from the enemy.

But something began to pull Samson's heart away from his consecration and dedication to God as a Nazarite. The flesh began to dominate his actions and feelings, and he yielded to the natural pleasures of the flesh more than to the Spirit of God that desired to use his life. Though Samson saw the many wonders of the Lord, as He granted him great deliverance from his enemies, his appreciation and love for the God of his father's began to wax cold. He began to look to himself as though he had done this great feat himself, and failed to give the Lord the glory. He began to say of how he had slain a thousand men, rather than thank the Lord for the great miracle God had performed through his life.

It is easy for our flesh to get caught up in itself, rather than yielding to the Holy Ghost that teaches us to deny ourselves. Jesus told the disciples to deny themselves, take up the cross and follow him. Even so are we commanded; to take up the cross as He did. Yet the cross, the emblem of suffering and shame, is many times overlooked, rejected, or even counted as an "outdated message", when it is truly the power of God unto salvation! The cross shows us that we must be crucified, and the old man must die so that the new man can live through the precious blood of Jesus. The cross is not pleasurable to the flesh, nor is it appealing to this generation, because everyone is looking for the easy way into heaven. The cross hurts: it is painful, until we reach the state of full submission to God, and the yielding of ourselves to His Holy Ghost. Jesus in all His teaching taught us to deny ourselves, to lay aside the weights and sins that beset us, and let the Spirit of God come alive in us. The spiritual life of truth, blessing and peace only come in a crucified life: a life committed and consecrated, sanctified and meet for the Master's use. Now we must measure and examine our lives to see if we are truly committed to him, as a surrendered crucified vessel that has died out to sin and the pleasures of the world. And we can do it, with the help of the Lord! We can't yield to the natural, and believe that we can do it without the Lord. Without Him we can do nothing!

Even though Samson failed to give the Lord glory as he should, the Lord still once again delivered him when he cried out to the Lord. The scripture says, *"And he was sore athirst, and called on the Lord, and said, Thou hast given this great deliverance into the hand of thy servant: and now shall I die for thirst, and fall into the hand of the uncircumcised? But God clave a hollow place that was in the jaw, and there came water thereout; and when he had drunk, his spirit came again, and he revived:"* (Judges 15:18-19)

Such great grace and mercy the Lord shows to us, even in our frailties, to grant deliverance to unworthy vessels that are only made worthy by the blood of Jesus! As we journey through this life of perils, we have to look around us and see the hand of the Lord at work in everything we do. And then, give Him the glory that he is so worthy of! To God be all the glory and honor, and thanksgiving and praise unto Jesus His Son! For the honor of His name, he delivers us and sets us free, that He might by glorified. Not in our own strength or power can we be free, nor survive in this world of wickedness and temptation without the Lord's mighty delivering hand. That glorious living water that flowed from a hollow place in that jawbone, gave life unto Samson, and his spirit came again and he revived! Revival comes when we give the Lord the glory and cry out to him for His great help. And as he moved upon Samson's life, so can He move in your situation today, breaking every bondage and hindrance, and giving you power over the enemy that is shouting against you. Claim your victory in Jesus, and see His mighty power come alive in your life!

Samson's failure came as he once again gave in to the seducing spirit of the Philistine women. A woman by the name of Delilah caught his attention. He was now met by the enemy of deception, an enemy that was truly roaring against him in the most subtle way. This enemy was not only going to harm his physical life, but his spiritual devotion to God as a Nazarite, consecrated for the service of the Lord. There are many times in this life that the devil, in the most subtle means, uses tactics and devices to steal, kill, and destroy us if possible. It is a great spirit of deception that has entered the world and caused many to be fooled by something that seems harmless. Who ever thought that the devil would use a woman to destroy this man of God, and bring him to his knees, when he was so mighty in strength and power, yet spiritually so weak and defenseless that he couldn't see the trap that was being set for him?

We must constantly be aware of that lion that roars against us, many times unawares, in the silence of deceit and lies, and in the persuasion of flesh and carnal appetites. The world has much to use to lure and deceive all that it can, and the devil with his mouth wide open is at the end waiting to devour every soul that he can. What can keep us from falling prey to this wicked enemy? Samson, in his great physical strength, was still being pulled into a trap that could have destroyed his eternal soul.

Be aware, brother and sister: Satan's tactics can pull you into a net that you can't get out of. There have been many that have started on the right way, desiring to be and do all they can for the Lord and His kingdom, only to end up in a trap that the enemy set for them. It sets their destiny on a downward spin toward destruction, and many times they are not able to pull out of it until it is too late. Though he roars with the fierceness to devour, the spirit of deception can close our ears to that roar, and blind our eyes to see and understand what is facing us. We fall prey as a bird in the snare to his devices, and many times without any remedy. Satan is lulling many to sleep, as Delilah did Samson, until she finally found the source of his great strength. Our strength in the Lord is certainly no secret to the enemy, but he knows exactly what to use to cause you to fall into his clenches.

Does he have a way to bring sin upon your life today? Have you found yourself in a spiritual slumber, that you can't seem to shake, and all the spiritual strength from the Lord has been pulled out of your soul, mind, and spirit? Is he using flesh and the carnal life to sap the very strength of the Spirit of God from your life? The scripture says, ***"And she made him sleep upon her knees; and she called for a man, and she caused him to shave off the seven locks of his head; and she began to afflict him, and his strength went from him. And she said, The Philistines be upon thee, Samson. And he awoke out of his sleep, and said, I will go out as at other times before, and shake myself. And he wist not that the***

Lord was departed from him." (Judges 16:19-20)

What an example this can be to us, for our teaching and learning; that we can be aware of our adversaries devices, and not fall into a place of spiritual slumber, blinded by the carnal passions of this life, and the cares of the world that can so easily lead us astray. The scripture says, *"Awake thou that sleepest, and arise from the dead, and Christ shall give thee light." (Ephesians 5:14)*

It is not the Lord's will for us to be put to sleep by the passions and appetites of the flesh. This strong man of God had been used mightily to display the power of the living God, and granted victory over the enemies of the Lord, was now being torn down by a spiritual lion that was greater than the beast that roared against him at Timnath. Now the devil had Samson right where he wanted him. There was no escaping without the loss of his eyes and the humiliation of the Philistine prison life. After the Philistines put out his eyes, he had not only been blinded spiritually by deception, but he lost his physical eye sight as well. The scriptures warn us many times of spiritual blindness, to not allow the devil to blind our eyes to his devices. But in the natural man, the weakness and frailties of the flesh cause us to become prey to his tricks. This is not an excuse for us to fail, but the sad truth that many are denying. We surrender to Satan's plan, rather than hold on to the truth that enlightens and delivers our spiritual soul. This does not have to be! We have been delivered by the blood of Jesus Christ from every device and work of the devil! The scripture says, ***"For this purpose was the Son of God manifested, that He might destroy the works of the devil." (1 John 3:8)*** His roar does not have to sting us with the deceitfulness of sin, and cause us to lose our victory and salvation in Christ Jesus! Today, we can take the authority over those things that have tried to blind and destroy us, and rather destroy those things so we can be free. Then in the end, we can rejoice that we held on to the promises of God, and look forward to the glorious return of Christ and that great resurrection day!

How glorious it would have been for Samson to have rejected the deceptive pull of the Philistine women, and said "no" to the silent roars of the enemy; and could he live to be able to be used to truly deliver the children of Israel from their enemies? Even now, the Lord searches our hearts and pleads with us that we would allow Him to take control, and give us power to fight the enemy, and take back the authority promised to us as the children of God! No Delilah should have the power over us, but the Lord is the victor, and we must allow Him to fight those battles for us to give us true victory, not defeat.

Because of his surrender to the wiles of the flesh, Samson became prisoner to the enemy, a display of shame and dishonor to the God of Israel. But in his time of suffering, as he was grinding in the prison house, he must have cried out to the Lord for mercy again. The scripture states that his hair began to grow again, and his state of mind began to regain strength in the Lord. Humbled by the loss of his eyes and his strength, he now realized that his only help was in the Lord. He could not fight his own battles anymore, but was now at the mercy of a God who had loved him and been with him from birth

The Lord knows the very plan for each one of our lives, and he is never taken by surprise as situations and circumstances arise. He many times directs our paths to bring us to the place of full surrender to him. Sometimes the loss of things, possessions, even family and friends brings us to a place of humility and surrender. There are times that even sickness and infirmities stricken our bodies to bring us to a place of surrender to the will of the Lord. It is not an intended hurt or inflicted suffering, but the plan of God to bring us to the place where we can be molded and prepared for the Master's use.

Who would have thought that Samson could be used again after he failed the Lord so miserably? This is not an excuse to sin, but a lesson to be heeded. Don't take for granted the great salvation given to us by God through His only begotten Son Jesus. Don't allow Satan to take your victory with the thought that it will be easily attained again. The devil is very deceptive and has many blinded by these types of false doctrines. We must remain faithful, holy, and true to the Lord that hath bought us with a price. The scripture in Romans six tells us: *"What shall we say then? Shall we continue in sin, that grace may abound? God forbid." (Romans 6:1-2)* This word teaches us that we cannot take grace for granted, or assume that the Lord has to tolerate or accept our sinful ways. He is a holy God, and He is just and true. He will judge and condemn sin, and deliver the righteous. Sin is not acceptable to Him, because He gave us Jesus to pay the price and deliver us from sin. Sin has its penalties, and holiness has its blessings. So avoid sin, say no to the enemy, and don't allow excuses for sin to separate us from the love of our God, and his Son Jesus.

The scripture tells us:*"And Samson called unto the LORD, and said, O Lord GOD, remember me, I pray thee, and strengthen me, I pray thee, only this once, O God, that I may be at once avenged of the Philistines for my two eyes. And Samson took hold of the two middle pillars upon which the house stood, and on which it was borne up, of the one with his right hand, and of the other with his left. And Samson said, Let me die with the Philistines. And he bowed himself with all his might; and the house fell upon the lords, and upon all the people that were therein. So the dead which he slew at his death were more than they which he slew in his life." (Judges 16:28-30)*

In closing this chapter of Samson's life, his cry for mercy obtained him another opportunity to defeat his enemies. The sad ending of his life came as he had to die with his enemies, rather than to gain victory and continue living for the Lord. As we stated before, it is truly a lesson to be learned, as we many times can feel that we are secure in what we have, only to so quickly have it taken from us, and be stripped of the spiritual life with God that has been given to us. Take this example; run from temptation and arm yourself with the full armor of God; don't allow the self-appetites of the flesh to rule your life and lead you away from the presence and gifts of God. Remember: *"The Lord knoweth how to deliver the godly out of temptations, and to reserve the unjust unto the day of judgment to be punished." (1 Peter 2:9)* Even as the Lord can deliver us from temptation, He can certainly deliver us from the clenches of the lion's mouth.

The promises of God are forever true to them that trust Him, but we must be faithful to what the Lord has called us to do. We must hold our standard, display the blood bought banner of Jesus, and preach His holy truth. As ministers, pastors, teachers, evangelists, whatever the call may be upon your life, do it to the fullest. Put away the "garment spotted by the flesh" and fulfill the plan of God for our lives. In doing so, we will truly find the sweetness in serving Jesus, as He so faithfully has saved us from all sin!

CHAPTER FOUR:

THE MAN OF GOD WHO CRIED AGAINST THE ALTAR AT BETHEL (1 KINGS 13)

"Cry aloud, spare not, lift up thy voice like a trumpet, and shew my people their transgression." (Isaiah 58:1)

The scriptures teach us many things as the Spirit of the Lord directs our hearts on this journey from earth to glory. One thing is certain; we can always find direction and examples of those who were blessed in their lives because of obedience to the word of the Lord. And then there were those who chose to disobey the commandment of the Lord and paid a severe penalty for their disobedience. In either case, the word of God provides us the opportunity to learn by the examples we read about. Making the right choices and decisions in this life will certainly affect our spiritual destiny, and pave the way to either eternal life forever with the Lord, or eternal destruction as penalty for our sin and unbelief. Therefore, our decisions and choices are very critical, as they can certainly affect us for the rest of our lives.

Let us now begin to explore the setting of this chapter, and the events that lead us to the character we are studying about in this chapter. This passage of scripture in 1 Kings thirteen tells us of a man of God who was sent by God to cry or pronounce judgment against the sins of an altar that was setup at Bethel by the king Jeroboam. It is not told in the scriptures where this man came from, (only that he was from the land of Judah), or any of his background, but that he was a man of God sent on a mission. A mission that would be critical to the future of a nation that was on very shaky ground. God had called Jeroboam to be king of the tribes of Israel when he took those tribes from under Rehoboam, Solomon's son. Jeroboam presumptuously disobeyed the Lord's commands, and caused the children of Israel to turn their hearts to idolatry, rather than leading them to the great God of Israel. Jeroboams' disobedience and sinful idolatry caused him to set up an altar with a golden calf at a place that had once been dedicated and consecrated unto the Lord. We can surely understand how displeasing this was to the Lord, after he had raised up Jeroboam to do his will and to lead his people in serving Him.

As our great Heavenly Father is so merciful, he chose a prophet, a man of God, to go and announce a prophetic cry against the altar as a warning to Jeroboam and the children of Israel. In an attempt to turn the hearts of the people, and cause them to repent of their idolatries, the prophetic cry rang through the ears of Bethel and those who were gathered to sacrifice at this idolatrous altar. The divinely anointed messenger is as bold as a lion (*Proverbs 28:1*), and is not to be intimidated by the fear of consequences.

Our Lord is always reaching out to His people, to turn their hearts back to him, and bring a reviving of the souls of men. He isn't willing that any should perish, but that all should come to repentance. Even so today, the Lord is searching for men and women of God that will be willing to stand in the gap for the souls of His people. The religious world today has sought after many gods, rather than to cling to our God Jehovah, and His Son Jesus. The imitation has taken the place of the real, and the true hunger for the truth and the Spirit of the Lord has been lost to every modern theme and marketing tactics to grow the crowd, instead of feeding the soul. When the blood of Jesus, and His great atonement for us on Calvary should be the center of our faith, it has been pushed aside to bring in many doctrines that can be classified as heresy by the Word of God. We don't speak this in criticism, but rather to expose the truth of the spiritual condition of the modern church today. It has reached a lukewarm state that is leading many souls astray rather than leading them back to the old fashioned altar of prayer and repentance. And we can see this is the reality that our nation's condition is so affected by the spiritual state of the church.

Once established upon Biblical principles, the commandments of God, and salvation by the precious blood of Jesus, our nation has become the place where everything goes, any kind of religion, no matter who or what is worshipped. This is the day when evil is called good, and good is called evil. When we can see the church of Satan growing in our nation, a country that once taught Biblical principles in government, education, and society, we know that there is definitely something wrong. When same sex marriage is approved, abortion laws passed, even the thought of transgender lifestyles taught to young children in our public schools, is there a man or woman who would say, "Lord send me!" Let me cry against the sins of the nation and pray that God would send revival here again! From our younger generations to our elders, there is a great need for revival in our land again. Only by prayer and fasting, turning from our selfish sinful ways, and finding our place at the feet of Jesus can this be possible. The Lord is looking for someone to take the burden, and desire to see revival come again in this last day. The devils' roar of sin and deceit is leading our nation astray, and only the power of God and deliverance through the blood of Jesus can bring a true change and true revival, beginning in the church.

Today's condition of our nation is very similar to the situation at the time of king Jeroboam, when God's people had once again gone astray from him. They began to seek other gods and ways that were so contrary to what the Lord had taught His people. In the great mercy and longsuffering of the King of glory for His people, he sent a man, to proclaim against the wrong, and warn of coming judgment, in an attempt to bring the peoples' hearts back to Himself. This warning came not only to the children of Israel, but to king Jeroboam himself as he sacrificed to the golden calves upon the altar. The scripture says, *"And he cried against the altar in the word of the Lord, and said, O altar, altar, thus saith the Lord; Behold a child shall be born unto the house of David, Josiah by name; and upon thee shall he offer the priest of the high places that burn incense upon thee, and men's bones shall be burnt upon thee." And, "Behold, the altar shall be rent, and the ashes that are upon it shall be poured out." (1 Kings 13:2-3)*

When Jeroboam heard the saying of the man of God, he cried out to lay hold on the prophet. When he did, his hand dried up that he couldn't pull it back again. Jeroboam's act of rebellion against the prophets' cry brought quick judgment, and the Lord showed him not to harm His prophet. To reject divine warnings aggravates transgression and invites vengeance. Disregard for God's warning and His word will not be tolerated, and quick judgment comes to those who despise the Word of God. His word is always quick and powerful, piercing to the soul. The prophets words came to pass as the altar was rent and the ashes poured out just as it was prophesied. Jeroboam quickly cried to the prophet to pray for him to the Lord to restore his hand to him, and as the man of God prayed, the Lord had mercy and restored his hand. Even in the disobedience of the king, the Lord was merciful to answer the man of God's prayer. How merciful and gracious is our Lord to those who will cry out to Him for mercy!

Then the testing for this great man of God began. King Jeroboam in gratitude invited the prophet to go home with him and refresh himself and he would give him a reward. Quickly, the man of God replied to the king, *"If thou wilt give me half thine house, I will not go in with thee, neither will I eat bread nor drink water in this place: For so it was charged me by the word of the Lord, saying, Eat no bread, nor drink water, nor turn again by the same way that thou camest. So he went another way, and returned not by the way that he came to Bethel."* *(1 Kings 13:8-10)* This was the command given to the prophet by the Lord when he was sent to deliver this message in Bethel. He wanted to be obedient unto the command of the Lord as a faithful servant to God. Our love for the Lord and His work does not exempt us from the fierce roar of temptation that the devil uses to cause us to disobey God's word and command. Temptation and trial testing is many times a daily occurrence in the life of a child of God, and as laborers for His kingdom, we can testify to this known truth.

Our theme throughout this study has been how to overcome and defeat the ugly spiritual lion that roars against us in many forms. In this chapter, he roared against the man of God through temptation: the temptation to disobey God's Word and commandment. Satan's deceptive lies have been at work since the beginning of creation, as we know that he beguiled Adam and Eve in the Garden of Eden. He many times will use tactics to cause us to think we are advantaged by doing the wrong, when we know that obedience is required by the God we serve. It is not always in the midst of the storm that the mariner finds his greatest danger, but in the deceitful and uncertain calm when some sudden and unexpected gust may strike his vessel unprepared.

The story was told of how the *Eurydice*, a noble British ship, after successfully navigating the world, was approaching the shores of England with every stitch of canvas spread, when her sails were smitten with a terrific blast, and in a few moments she reeled over and sank to the bottom of the sea, with hundreds of brave seamen whose hearts were beating with joy in the near prospect of home!

We many times think that temptation only comes to those who don't live for the Lord, or the spiritually weak and weary. But it comes to those who are in places of spiritual leadership and authority in the church. It comes even to those who themselves proclaim, preach, teach, study, and even live the Word of God in their everyday lives. Warning is given through the scripture that says *"Wherefore let him that thinketh he standeth take heed lest he fall." (1 Corinthians 10:12)* This warning that Paul wrote to the church at Corinth was letting God's people know that they were going to be tempted; tempted to provoke and disobey the Lord. As the children of Israel provoked the Lord in the wilderness, and gave us the example that we should not fall into the same snare of the enemy that roars against our souls through the enticement of temptation. The scripture continues and says, *"There hath no temptation take you but such as is common to man: but God is faithful who will not suffer you to be tempted above that ye are able; but will with the temptation also make a way to escape, that ye may be able to bear it." (1 Corinthians 10:13)*

This promise lets us know that no matter how severe the temptation or how fierce the roar of that lion of temptation is against us, our God can still deliver us! Calling upon Jesus, and holding to his unchanging hand will bring us through every trial testing time! Although the Lord limits our temptation and can make a way of escape, we still must face and overcome our own temptation. This is only possible with a prayer life and communion with the Holy Ghost that will give us power over sin and the temptation to sin. It was once written by a great preacher of our times, *"The holy man is not one who cannot sin; a holy man is one who will not sin."* That is such a profound truth; to be holy is not because we can't fall to sin, it is that we choose to not to fall to sin.

The book of James also admonishes us with a promise: *"Blessed is the man that endureth temptation: for when he is tried, he shall receive the crown of life, which the Lord hath promised to them that love him." (James 1:12)* So we understand that there is a great blessing that we are promised when we endure that great roar of temptation from the adversary, and still hold to our faith and commitment to the one that saved us. What a promise, to receive a great crown of life, that the Lord has promised to each one that loves Him enough to say "Lord, I will hold on to your promises through temptation and trial, and obey your Holy Word!" It takes fighting one battle at a time, one temptation at a time, and asking the Lord for the strength to overcome at that moment that is most critical. James also tells us; *"My brethren, count it all joy when ye fall into divers temptations; Knowing this, that the trying of your faith worketh patience." (James 1:2-3)* The blessing of having joy in the midst of temptation, is only realized when we see the growth of our faith and patience as we endure the temptation. Then are we proven to be the vessel the Lord's want us to be, and our joy is made full by the help of the Holy Ghost in the midst of the trial. We need His help desperately as we face the fierce roar of the enemy.

This man of God we are studying faced the stages of temptation from the greatest sources: a king and another prophet. The tempter that roared against him used the tactics that are common to each and every temptation and trial we face. We can make note of these steps of temptation that try to bring us to failure in our walk with the Lord, and pray that the Lord will strengthen us against the roars and attacks of the enemy. James once again explains the process of temptation and the results thereof. We read in James 1:14-15 *"But every man is tempted, when he is drawn away of his own lust and enticed. Then when lust hath conceived, it bringeth forth sin: and sin, when it is finished, bringeth forth death."* This is the pattern that temptation takes as it roars against the soul of man. Therefore we need the armor of God to equip us and prepare us for battle so that we are not overtaken by temptation and sin.

We see that the man of God was not deceived by the temptation of king Jeroboam inviting him to his house, because the word of God was fresh in his soul and mind, and he knew he must obey. But as many times we can become complacent, and overcome with the natural elements of life: the appetites of the flesh become more appealing to us than obedience to the Word of God. And if our spiritual roots of faith and power in the Holy Ghost aren't alive and active in our lives, we are drawn away of our own lust and enticed. As exhaust, weariness, and hunger began to set in, it could have become difficult to refuse the comforts of the flesh. Weary and faint as he must have been with his journey, this invitation would cost the prophet some self-denial to resist. Satan ever tempts us at our weakest point and weakest moment. We must constantly be aware and do as Jesus commanded us, *"Watch and pray"*. When we find ourselves in that place of trial, we must know that we cannot yield to the forces of the adversary, nor bow to his intimidating roar of temptation that can cause us to fall into the trap the devil has set for us.

This man of God that had obeyed the voice of the Lord, and was used mightily to bring a message to the king of Israel, was being led into a snare of temptation he did not expect. He overcame the first test, and resisted the desire to join the king, and held onto the commandment of the Lord who had sent him. It was a deceitful attempt to the man of God under the kings' evil influence. But he conquered that temptation, and maybe expected it to come from a king that wasn't God fearing, nor serving the Lord he knew as God. He was tempted with royal hospitality, a reward, and physical refreshment. But now as he journeyed on, he never expected another great temptation to come to him in such a deceiving way. We must constantly be on our guard to not be deceived.

In this day of great deception in our land, the influence that Satan has upon many lives through the many means of deception is overwhelming the multitudes, and the enemies roar of temptation is leading many into the terrible consequences of sin and destruction: not only by spiritual death, but even physical death. That is why Paul the apostle wrote in the third chapter of second Timothy, *"This know also, that in the last days perilous times shall come." (2 Timothy 3:1)* This gives us warning that we are living in the days of great peril, not only physically, but spiritual perils that endanger the soul. Our soul is at stake every time we submit to temptation, rather than overcome and defeat temptation. It is true that the perils of trial testing will come, but how we handle and conquer those temptations will determine the future of our spiritual walk with the Lord, and even in eternity. Our desire is to not fail Him, but to trust Him, knowing that He is our deliverer; the one that can still deliver us out of the mouth of the lion!

At that moment the man of God felt very confident that he had fulfilled God's will, but little did he expect the temptation that would prove to be his ruin that came so unexpectedly. And it came from an unexpected source: another prophet! One who for some reason was purposed to find and cause this man of God to fail in obeying the Lord's command. This prophet in Bethel was told the full account by his sons that were apparently present when he prophesied against the altar at Jeroboams' sacrifice. This was surely a sign that this prophet of Bethel was well aware of the idolatry and sins of the wicked king, and yet had failed to allow the Lord to use him to bring the message against the abominations of the king. We are not sure of his motives or intentions, but we do know that being told of his sons what this man of God had done, he pursued quickly to find the man. Many times there are those, who in their deceived minds, become envious of someone that is being used by the Lord, and they seek to destroy that person, just for carnal motives that please and glorify the flesh. They will do anything they can to gain a position of authority, not concerned of who is destroyed and hurt in the process. This seems to be the case with this prophet from Bethel.

Taking the same path the man of God had journeyed, he came and found the man of God stopped along the road. The scripture says, *"And went after the man of God, and found him sitting under an oak: and he said unto him, Art thou the man of god that camest from Judah? And he said, I am. The he said unto him, Come home with me, and eat bread." (1 Kings 13:14-15)*

It would be good for us to take note of this situation. We can see that if we don't continue on our journey but stop along the way, we can be overtaken by the temptation of the enemy. The man of God, weary from his journey, and having neither eaten nor drank anything, was taking a much needed rest. But there are times when we spiritually take a rest, yet we need not to become slothful, nor allow the devil to catch us idle along this path to glory. Remember, Satan will always seek to catch us at our weakest point and our weakest moment. This happened to this man of God

As the servants of the Lord, in ministry, leadership, or a member of the church, we have a great calling that is given to us. As the Word of God speaks to us, and the Holy Ghost leads us into the calling of God, we must never take this journey lightly, nor allow ourselves to fall into a spiritual slumber and sleep. That is when the lion of temptation will roar against us in a very deceptive way, and we can be overtaken by sin. Disobedience: it caused Adam and Eve to be put out of the Garden of Eden, and the curse of death to come upon mankind, and it takes on many hidden forms to come upon us quickly and catch us off guard.

His first defense to the prophet of Bethel was "no, I will not disobey the word of the Lord". He once again quoted to the prophet from Bethel the words that the Lord had commanded him. It seemed they became as meaningless words, overcome by the words of persuasion that seemed to roar louder than the still small voice of the spirit of God that commissioned him. We can testify of the goodness of the Lord, and the faith we have in him, but if we don't hold true to our testimony, our faith is overturned and we fall prey to sin. Those words of deceptive comfort and rest began to sound good to the man of God, as the prophet from Bethel told him, *"I am a prophet also as thou art; and an angel spake unto me by the word of the Lord, saying, Bring him back with thee into thine house, that he may eat bread and drink water. But he lied unto him. (1Kings 13:18)* Today, many are being put to sleep by that same spirit of deception, when we must stay aware and be sober, watching and praying always

Let us reflect on the theme of our study: *"Be sober, be vigilant; because your adversary the devil, as a roaring lion, walketh about, seeking whom he may devour:"* (1 Peter 5:8) Now we come to the part of this chapter that made the difference between life and death for this man of God, not only spiritually, but physically also. This prophet from Bethel, though claiming the office of a prophet, was used by the devil to lie to this man of God, and deceive him into disobeying the command that came directly from the Lord himself. The prophet of Bethel said, (as a lion roars against his prey), an angel told him to bring him back to his house, to feed him and give him drink: speaking the greatest lie and deceptive words to steal this man's victory he had gained in his obedience to God at the altar in Bethel. Disobedience was drawing him into a net of deception, to destroy the good he had accomplished when he fulfilled his prophetic mission at Bethel. The prophet was tempted with three things: hospitality, refreshment, and reward.

The devil seeks to do the same to every one of God's children. Many times we do our best to obey the Lord, his word and his commands, keeping our lives clean from sin. But then the lions' roar of temptation comes against us, and we feel that we have done enough, and we can become relaxed in what we know as the truth. Deception comes, pulls us into a net of disobedience, and causes a break in the relationship between us and our heavenly Father. Even as in this day when faith is being fought on every hand, and false teachings and doctrines are arising that tear down the blood bought redemptive power of the blood of Jesus, His atonement for sin at Calvary, His healing power, His resurrection, His soon return, and His call for repentance and holy living in the church. It is certainly the last "perilous" times that Paul the apostle wrote about, and the fulfillment of the scripture when Jesus said, *"For there shall arise false Christs, and false prophets, and shall shew great signs and wonders; insomuch that, if it were possible, they shall deceive the very elect." (Matthew 24:24)*

Many in our church world are being deceived into believing that they can live any lifestyle and still enter God's holy heaven. They believe that the Lord overlooks sin, and is obligated to forget our disobedient and stubborn ways, when His word says the complete opposite. He said, *"there shall in no wise enter into it anything that defileth, neither whatsoever worketh abomination, or maketh a lie: but they which are written in the Lamb's book of life. (Revelation 21:27)* By these words in the scripture, we know that God means business, and He will not tolerate disobedience. The enemy knows this and will do everything he can to cause us to fall if possible.

Finally, the persuasion of the old prophet, and the lying spirit of deception caused the man of God to yield to the temptation. And as we read in the book of James, lust conceived, and it brought forth sin. The man of God, instead of continuing on his journey following the Lord, turned and followed the lying mouth of a lying deceptive spirit working through a wolf in sheep's clothing back to his home in Bethel.

As they sat to eat bread at the table, the word of the Lord came to the prophet that brought him back to eat with him. The scripture says, *"And he cried unto the man of God that came from Judah, saying, thus saith the Lord, Forasmuch as thou hast disobeyed the mouth of the Lord, and hast not kept the commandment which the Lord thy God commanded thee, But camest back, and hast eaten bread and drunk water in the place, of the which the Lord did say to thee, Eat no bread, and drink no water; thy carcase shall not come unto the sepulcher of thy fathers." (1 Kings 13:21-22)*

A pronouncement of judgment came for this man who in the beginning, obeyed the Lord, yet at the end, disobeyed. A thought should stir us at this moment: Jesus said, *"He that endureth to the end, the same shall be saved." (Matthew 10:22)* This is those that through trial and tribulation, even temptation, hold on to the truth and obey it as well, will be saved in the end. Not those who begin the race, but those who fight this good fight of faith to the very end. Though the man of God had performed and obeyed the Lord in pronouncing judgment at Bethel, in his disobedience he was caught and found guilty, and thereby condemned himself to judgment and death. The word said that his *"carcass"* would not come to the sepulchers of his fathers, showing that he would never make it back home. What a sad ending for a man who was used by the Lord in such a mighty way!

Now we can think of how many people in this day and time start on the right path and are saved to good works, living a right life. But when temptation comes they are caught off guard, lose their hold on salvation and are caught speechless. This man of God is not quoted as saying anything to the message that came from the prophet of Bethel, because he knew his guilt could not be hid. He had disobeyed the one that loved him enough to choose him, and use him for the work of the Lord. That spiritual lion of deception roared against him with enticing words, bringing him to a place of complete disobedience to God's word. We must take caution, and know that we are not invincible to the power and temptation of the lying spirit of deception that is working in the world. Even now, as the epistles of John speak, there are many antichrists in the world, deceiving and destroying many by their lying words. But the Lord is still faithful to keep those who will hold on, and not yield to the persuasion of the enemy. Don't be deceived by fair, flattering words of deception that come roaring out of that spiritual lions' mouth to cause you to surrender to his wicked persuasion. Don't give in when the enemy roars against you to take you away from what you know is true in God's Word. Always remember, the Lord will not go against His Word. And as Paul the apostle preached to the Galatians, he warned of this kind of deception. ***"But though we, or an angel from heaven, preach any other gospel unto you than that which we have preached unto you, let him be accursed." (Galatians 1:8)*** Paul then repeated the statement again giving witness to not receive any other gospel, any other message, than what is written in God's Holy Word. Even if an angel comes, and brings you a message that goes against

God's word, we must know it is Satan transformed into an angel of light.

We must face that lying roar of deception even as Jesus did when he faced the devil's temptation in the wilderness. We see that Jesus used the Word of God, not only to answer the devils temptations, but also to overcome those temptations. We must rely on the power of the Holy Ghost and the truth of God's Word to see the victory come. We can overcome these lying temptations that come our way, and take this example to heart, believing that the Lord can deliver us. Paul the apostle wrote to Timothy his son in the faith and said, *"Fight the good fight of faith, lay hold on eternal life, whereunto thou art also called...".* *(1 Timothy 6:12)* Remember, with God, all things are possible, and we don't have to fall into the snares of deception. We can be strong in the Lord, and in the power of His might, as we are clothed with the full armor of God.

We now look at what followed, as the prophet of Bethel set the man of God on his own donkey, and sent him on his journey; a journey that would lead to his demise. Such a sad ending to what could have been a glorious outcome, as comes from being obedient to the Lord we serve. We are not told any details of the conversation between the two prophets, neither of any words of sorrow or concern from the man of God as he was found guilty of disobedience. Could it have been that in his shame, he didn't feel it necessary to repent and make things right with the

Lord who had called him to such a great work? Could it have been that he felt the Lord would overlook his wrong, and accept him as he was? We know that sin, when it is not repented of will surely lead to certain death: spiritual death, as well as physical death. Once again referring to the Book of James chapter one, verse fifteen: *"Then when lust hath conceived, it bringeth forth sin: and sin when it is finished, bringeth forth death."* This was the outcome for this man of God who chose to disobey the word of the Lord. His disobedience was now leading him down a road toward death.

The scripture says, *"and when he was gone, a lion met him by the way, and slew him: and his carcase was cast in the way". (v.24)* It goes on to say, *"and when the prophet that brought him back from the way heard thereof, he said, It is the man of God, who was disobedient unto the word of the Lord: therefore the Lord that delivered him unto the lion, which hath torn him, and slain him, according to the word of the Lord, which he spake unto him."(v.26)* This study is called *"When God Shuts the Lion's Mouth"*. We may think- why didn't the Lord deliver this man from the treacherous roar of that lion that took his life? What happened? Even though he had done great things for the Lord, yet he was destroyed by a lion along his journey home?

The consequences of disobedience are great!

1. Adam and Eve were put out of the Garden of Eden because of disobedience to God's command. Their

sin brought the curse of death upon all mankind. (Genesis 3:23-24)

2. Lot's wife was turned to a pillar of salt because she disobeyed the command of the Lord and looked back to Sodom. (Genesis 19:26)

3. Many of the children of Israel didn't enter the promised-land because of unbelief and disobedience. Even Moses wasn't allowed to enter the promised-land because he disobeyed the Lord. (Numbers 27:14)

4. Nadab and Abihu lost their lives because of disobedience to the Lord in the service of the priesthood. They offered a strange fire before the Lord which he had commanded them not to do. (Leviticus 10:1)

5. Achan and his family lost their lives because of his disobedience to God's law, and his coveting the spoils of the enemy in the book of Joshua.

(Joshua 7:24-26)

6. Eli lost his sons and the ark of God to the enemy, and his life because he disobeyed the Lord in allowing his son's to despise the offerings of the people, and commit carnal sins in the tabernacle of the Lord. (1 Samuel 4:17-18)

7. King Saul's disobedience caused him to lose the kingdom, and also to be rejected by the Lord who took His spirit from him. (1 Samuel 15:18-23)

8. Judas disobeyed the Lord by betraying Jesus for

thirty pieces of silver. The guilt of his disobedience and betrayal drove him to suicide. (Matthew 27:3-5)

These are just a few examples in the scriptures of where disobedience to God's Word can take us. It always brings forth death, spiritually and physically.

When we look at the situation of the man of God and his disobedience, it is an example of how sometimes our pride gets in our way of admitting our wrongs, and stops us from humbling ourselves before the Lord. There are other examples in the Bible of those who disobeyed the Lord, but in the humility of repentance, turned back to the Lord for mercy, found their grace in the time of need, and the Lord pardoned their sin.

This is the instrument the Lord uses to shut the lion's mouth and brings deliverance to the child of God! There is a place to find mercy and grace thru confessing our sin and sincerely repenting for our wrongs and our disobedience to the Lord. If we just humble ourselves under the mighty hand of God that he may exalt us to His righteousness and save us from the curse of death. This man's death was so unnecessary, if he only would have turned and repented to the Lord for his disobedience, what a different outcome this story would have had. It left this man of God with a name of "disobedient" instead of the name of "obedient" to the word of the Lord. Throughout Biblical history, this story has been given to us as a man that was used of the Lord became disobedient, and fell prey to a lion's death trap, as he roared against him in death. But even in his death, the Lord was merciful and didn't allow the lion to destroy his body, which was not common for a hungry young lion. It normally would have devoured his prey, even the donkey too.

The mercy of the Lord is to those who will call upon Him, seek Him with a whole heart, repent and turn from our wicked and disobedient ways, believing Him for forgiveness and salvation. He came to seek and to save that which was lost, and when we live in disobedience we are lost without him, and need to be saved and delivered. The wicked roar of a lion of disobedience is roaring against God's people today, seeking to devour whom he can. But we do not have to lose the battle to temptation; we can fight to do right, hold on to the truth, and obey the commands of the Lord even when it is a great sacrifice. Always remember, obedience is better than to sacrifice! It always pays to obey the voice of the Lord.

In closing this chapter, let us take some time to consider our spiritual condition in the Lord. In honesty, search our hearts to make sure that we are not found in disobedience to the Lord's word. Maybe he has called you, chosen you for his service, but the sacrifice of commitment to His work seems greater than we can attain. We must know that we can make it and *"do all things through Christ which strengeneth us"!* We can obey his voice, and still hold on to His truth and commands, when everyone else is telling us "you don't have to live that strict way", or "you can live your life as you please and still be saved", when we know the Word of God says different.

Take this opportunity now to do some true soul searching: find your place at the feet of Jesus in repentance for any disobedience that might be found in our lives. Allow the Lord to use His gift of repentance and mercy to bring us back to our first works, in obedience to God's word. Let us ponder the words Jesus spoke to the church at Ephesus in Revelation chapter two: ***"Nevertheless I have somewhat against thee, because thou hast left thy first love. Remember therefore from whence thou art fallen, and repent, and do the first works; or else I will come unto thee quickly, and will remove thy candlestick out of his place, except thou repent."(v.4-5)*** A cry of truth, yet a cry of mercy, to bring His church back into obedience. His grace and mercy is constantly seeking to reach us in our times of fault and failure, not willing that we fall into the snares of guilt and condemnation brought about by disobedience to God's word. It is possible for us to be obedient, willing, and faithful to follow in His blessed footsteps that have been laid before us. Now, it is up to us to allow the Lord to shut the lion's mouth for you, and help you to get to the place you need to be. Find your place of safety in the loving arms of Jesus, and allow him to keep you from all harm.

CHAPTER FIVE:
DANIEL – "A MAN OF EXCELLENT SPIRIT & WISDOM"

"Then this Daniel was preferred above the presidents and princes, because an excellent spirit was in him;" (Daniel 6:3)

We will now study and explore the life of a man who chose to serve God and believe God when all the odds were against him. In our previous chapters, we have studied others who stood tests of faith and persecution, but certainly the book of Daniel gives us some great Biblical truths that righteousness and steadfastness in the way of the Lord are rewarded by God's divine intervention. We have some of the historic accounts of Daniel's life given to us in the book of Daniel, from his youth to his elder years. These accounts are great testimonies of how faith can be tried and tested, as well as the perils and dangers of persecution in a strange land, physically as well as spiritually.

As a young man, Daniel was exposed to several traumatic and perilous experiences in his early life. Being a young Jew at the time of the carrying away of the Jews to Babylon, Daniel was one of many younger males who found himself prey to the rule of a king who did not regard the God of His fathers. Daniel's faith in his God was going to be tested and tried under the hand of a ruthless leader whose desire was to indoctrinate and brainwash the young Jews into the worship of his gods and the wicked lifestyles of the Babylonians. Daniel's faith was going to be tested by the roar of a spiritual lion who sat on a throne and did not regard the life of the young or old. And as he was being prepared for service to this ungodly king, there was a God in heaven who would prove to be faithful to him in every trial and test as he grew into the man God wanted him to be.

As we study Daniels life, we would like to encourage young people who are being faced with the persuasion and roars of the deceptive spirit and teachings that are filling the minds and hearts of young people in the public school, and in secular social media platforms. The similarities in what was happening to the young Jews in Daniels' day follow the same satanic pattern that we see in today's society. Socialistic agendas to brainwash our young people into the servitude of the state, rather than to be servants of the living God are alive and well and being promoted in the educational systems of today. From elementary to college curriculum, the teachings of evolution, atheism, humanism, critical race theory, trans-gender lifestyles, and non-biblical world views are being pounded into this generation that could prove to be the last generation. Young people are becoming "social media addicts", not being able to break the vicious cycle of evil and sin being fed to them these media platforms. Our young people are being exposed to teachings that will erase any thought of the God of heaven and His Son Jesus out of the hearts and minds of every child, boy or girl, and be replaced with the ungodly teachings that lead our young generation to a place of destruction. But as that spiritual lion of deception was not able to persuade a young man with a steadfast heart, we can also help and encourage our young generation to hold onto the sound Biblical teachings of the Gospel, the salvation thru the blood of Jesus, and deliverance from the world of evils that surround them every day.

Daniel was given great wisdom and understanding by the spirit of the Lord, which gained him great favor in the Babylonian kingdom. His knowledge and understanding exceeded many others, being instructed in the wisdom of the Chaldeans. It gained him recognition of the Babylonian and Persian kings, and also by the Almighty in the Holy Scriptures, where the king of Tyrus is referred to as being "wiser than Daniel". He was also referred to in the class of "Noah and Job" in the book of Ezekiel. He also prophesied of the coming Messiah, of which prophecies the Lord Jesus fulfilled to the exact timing as spoken by Lord through Daniel. The Lord recognized him as being a man of wisdom. This God given wisdom and ability led Daniel through many trials and tests that came his way, and gave him the ability to prophesy future events with great accuracy.

Though there were many great testimonies recorded in Daniel's life, we are going to concentrate on the sixth chapter of the book of Daniel as our study in this chapter. This chapter will continue the theme of our study, *"When God Shuts the Lions Mouth"*.

The sixth chapter of Daniel begins in the latter part of

Daniels life when the Persian king Darius had taken the kingdom. Daniel had served under king Nebuchadnezzar, Evil-Merodach and Belshazzar: and when the kingdom was now taken over by the Medes and Persians, Daniel was still in a place of service under the new king.

The scripture tells us in Daniel chapter six:

"It pleased Darius to set over the kingdom an hundred and twenty princes, which should be over the whole kingdom; And over these three presidents; of whom Daniel was first: that the princes might give accounts unto them, and the king should have no damage. Then this Daniel was preferred above the presidents and princes, because an excellent spirit was in him; and the king thought to set him over the whole realm. Then the presidents and princes sought to find occasion against Daniel concerning the kingdom; but they could find none occasion nor fault; forasmuch as he was faithful, neither was there any error or fault found in him."

(Daniel 6:1-4)

As we can see by these scriptures, Daniel had favor with the new monarch as well as the former kings because of his excellent spirit, and the close relationship he had with the Lord. This relationship with the God of Israel kept Daniel innocent and without fault or error. Daniel was placed in a position above his peers, which we know caused much malice and envy against this prophet of God; especially amongst those of another nation. We know by reading the previous chapters that Daniel had already been used in mighty ways by the Lord to astonish the Babylonians, interpreting dreams, prophesying and revealing the secrets of the heart to the former kings. Now, the divine favor shown upon Daniel would prove to promote him in the new Persian kingdom.

But there were going to be some obstacles for Daniel, even as it is for us in our walk with the Lord. We know that we will not grow in the Lord's favor without our faith and endurance being tried. In this Christian walk, the Lord desires to exalt us in his favor. But opposition is sure to come and test our faithfulness to the Lord. The scripture tells us in James 5:10: *"Take, my brethren, the prophets, who have spoken in the name of the Lord, for an example of suffering affliction, and of patience".*

In order to grow in the kingdom of God and in His favor, suffering and persecution is almost certain to prove our faithfulness to the Lord that saved us. We have spoken extensively about testing and temptation in the previous chapter, and it was proven so in Daniel's life; it was no different. Whether young or old, as we are called into the service of the Lord, and the Lord begins to prepare us for his service, we will be fought. Persecution, both spiritually and physically will find its way onto our path, to try to hinder, stop, and destroy our faithfulness to the Lord if possible. We must persist to hold onto the truth, and be faithful in all the Lord has called us to do, regardless of the cost. Through insult and injury, the devil seeks to cause us to fall from our faithfulness to the Lord. But Daniel is a great example to us that we can still hold onto our integrity, even when Satan is saying ***"touch all that he hath, and he will curse thee to thy face. (Job 1:11)*** We know that the devil is the accuser of the brethren, and he will bring accusation and condemnation, but in our innocence and humility before the Lord, He will exalt us in due season.

Daniels faithfulness, integrity, and honesty were going to be used against him by these other presidents and princes whose envy drove them to use whatever means they could to have him removed from his authority. Political power and deceptive persuasion were used by these men to bring an accusation against Daniel. And they could only find his faith and belief in his God, and his obedience to the law of his God as a source to use against him. Realizing this, they devised a plan that would use Darius' own laws to have Daniel convicted and sentenced to death.

The same wickedness and deceitful persuasion that is working in the world today to destroy every child of God that holds faithful to the truth of God's word, was used to bring an accusation against a man of God who loved his Lord with all his heart. We can look at Daniels boldness and courage to hold on and stand against even what was deemed "civil law" of that day, and take the example he gave us; to follow the spirit of the Lord that leads us into all His truth. We need faith, courage, and boldness so desperately to be able to fulfill the will of God in our lives. In these days where the civil laws of the land are no longer Bible based, or based on the freedoms that our nation was founded on, we are going to have very similar situations confront us. We must take a bold stand for what we believe, and know that the God that saved us is also able to deliver us.

King Darius was approached by the princes in the scripture, and they persuaded him against Daniel: *"All the presidents of the kingdom, the governors, and the princes, the counsellors, and the captains, have consulted together to establish a royal statute, and to make a firm decree, that whosoever shall ask a petition of any God or man for thirty days, save of thee, O king, he shall be cast into the den of lions. Now, O king, establish the decree, and sign the writing, that it be not changed, according to the law of the Medes and Persians, which altereth not. Wherefore king Darius signed the writing and the decree."* (Daniel 6:7-9)

Some have thought, how could such a decree been made into law by a king who knew this would affect Daniel, his most loyal president? Daniel had been faithful to king Darius. But in blind persuasion, not thinking of anyone but himself, he was lifted up in his heart to think that no man would ask anything of any god or man, but only of him. This prideful arrogance and deception caused him to enact a law that was aimed directly at the man God had placed in his kingdom as a great asset; the man named Daniel. As they say, "ambition knows no boundaries", and these leaders that were gathered together against Daniel didn't care who this law would affect, as long as it accomplished their evil intentions: to bring about the demise of the man of God they envied so greatly.

This brings us to a point we would like to make in this chapter: political objectives that have evil motives are used by the devil to destroy many lives. Those who pass these laws do not consider the overall effects of what or who will be harmed in the process of passing corrupted laws. Laws have been passed legalizing abortion, same sex marriages, making marijuana a legal drug, etc., and they affect so many lives bringing them to eternal destruction. This is why our governments have become so corrupted, because they use any means to accomplish only what profits the politicians and their parties, not considering the benefit or well-being of the nation. America has allowed politics and political parties to rule, rather than the Lord who gave us the Biblical principles our nation was founded upon. Deception, envy, and power struggles are the center of our government, rather than the welfare of the people that the government is elected to serve. But we have our eyes upon the Lord for our direction, to be our supplier in the times of need. We cannot rely upon government, secular outlets, the media, or even our modern health systems. We must keep our eyes on

Jesus as the author and finisher of our faith, and know that he will not fail us in our times of need. He will not fail to help us if we continue to trust Him for all things.

Now, the roar of a spiritual lion of accusation roared against Daniel, as the kings decree was signed into law, and could not be changed according to the laws of the Medes and Persians. Daniel, as soon as he knew the writing was signed by the king into law, went to his room as his custom was, opened his windows toward Jerusalem, and prayed and gave thanks three times a day as before. We may think that this was an act of civil disobedience: but Daniel knew that he was not to dishonor his God by obeying the laws of the ungodly that would stop him from praying to the God of heaven. He would continue in his worship and praise to the one he served, and would obey "God rather than men". Even so must we be bold and courageous to stand against evil and carry the banner of the Gospel of Jesus Christ, declaring His atoning plan of salvation for all mankind. We maybe falsely accused, persecuted for our faith and stand for the Gospel, but it will be worth it all when we see Jesus!

Daniel also knew that his prayers and communion with the Lord would bring him through whatever he had to face. Of course, the men who had devised this plan against Daniel were waiting for him to break the law of the king so they could bring an accusation against him. And so it was, when they gathered and found Daniel praying, they brought it before king Darius. The lion of deceptive accusation roared against Daniel and accused him of dishonoring the law of the king. They even used the kings own words to cause him to agree that anyone asking petition of any god or man would be cast into the lion's den. The scripture says, *"Then answered they and said before the king, That Daniel, which is of the children of the captivity of Judah, regardeth not thee, O king, nor the decree that thou hast signed, but maketh his petition three times a day. Then the king, when he heard these words, was sore displeased with himself, and set his heart on Daniel to deliver him: and he laboured till the going down of the sun to deliver him. (Daniel 6:14-15)*

When the enemy the devil, chooses to accuse and destroy, he holds no bounds or limits, he does it to the fullest. He comes as that roaring lion, *"seeking whom he may devour."* Daniel was the object of this plot of evil, and they were not going to be satisfied until he was destroyed. But they were forgetting that the God that Daniel prayed to everyday was not going to allow that roar of accusation to destroy Daniel. What Daniel was going thru was going to be used for the glory of God, and the Lord would once again show his mighty power of deliverance for the man of God who trusted him. Could the king have delivered him from this plot of evil that had been devised against him? It's very possible. But, the Lord had a plan to show forth his glory in Daniel's deliverance, not by the hand of man, but by the hand of God.

Now consider this in your life: we are not going to get thru this life without being tested. Our faith will be tried: whether we are in ministry, or just a child of God in the church, we will not escape this roar of the devils' accusation and trying of our faith. It is going to come, regardless of who we are. The scripture in Peter tells us in 1 Peter 1:7: *"That the trial of your faith, being much more precious than of gold that perisheth, though it be tried with fire, might be found unto praise and honour and glory at the appearing of Jesus Christ:"* Also he tells us in 1 Peter 4:1: *"Forasmuch then as Christ hath suffered for us in the flesh, arm yourselves likewise with the same mind: for he that hath suffered in the flesh hath ceased from sin;"*

We can see by this exhortation from the apostle Peter that we are going to suffer the fires of persecution and testing, and spiritual attacks which would like to destroy the relationship we have with the Lord, seeking to destroy our foundation of faith we have in Him. But if we hold on to the end, we shall come forth as pure gold. The book of Job said it well: *"But he knoweth the way that I take: when he hath tried me, I shall come forth as gold." (Job 23:10)* He knows what we are facing and what we have to go through; and He is able to help us in our times of need, being our faithful High Priest.

Daniel could have become very dismayed by what was happening, knowing that he was innocent of the things they were accusing him of. His faith could have been shaken: doubt and fear could have filled his heart not knowing how things were going to turn out. He could have tried to find help in another person, friend or family, but he took his courage in the Lord that he knew could deliver him from any evil plan that was devised against him. No matter what king or leader comes against us, persons of high standing and power in society, we look to the scripture that tells us *"Greater is he that is in you than he that is in the world."(1 John 4:4)* This is what Daniel was holding on to, knowing that his God was able to do all things.

Daniels godly character, integrity and his strong prayer life kept him from doubting the God of his fathers, and from yielding to the lies of deceptive accusation that had come against him. This was something that was only accomplished through those special prayer times that Daniel had with our heavenly Father, as he held faithful to his time in the presence of the Lord.

Our prayer life is so vital to our spiritual survival! Times of prayer, seeking the Lord with a sincere heart, humble and broken before him, will give us the strength we need to face these trials. The Lord Jesus, being our greatest example, showed us the power of prayer in the many times he would "continue all night in prayer". Also, in the garden of Gethsemane, as he prayed to the Father, He received the spiritual strength He needed to be the great sacrifice for mankind. We will speak more of that in the next chapter. Many of our battles are fought on our knees in prayer, and in our waiting upon the Lord for his help. Only He can keep us through trying perilous times in our lives, and in times of betrayal by our closest acquaintances. Daniel could have retaliated against the accusations; he could have tried to make excuse or defend himself. But he chose to fall on his knees before a merciful God that He believed would fight for him, even when all the odds were against him. Always remember – our God is merciful, man is not. Repeating, many times man has no mercy, but the Lord is merciful.

This is such a great example for us, even in the days we are living in. We are fought and accused, and Satan's deceptive practices come thru many forms to try to deceive and destroy: but falling on our knees three times a day as Daniel did will help to keep us and give us strength through these perils and trials. This great meekness was a virtue that Daniel needed in that hour. Always remember, the battle is not ours, it is the Lord's!

Then came the true test of Daniel's faith in the God he served. The accusation could not be denied because Daniel would not deny praying to the Lord he loved, and he was willing to suffer the consequences, knowing that the eternal reward of suffering for righteousness was worth it all. All the earthly rewards could not compare to the eternal rewards of glory that wait for those who sacrifice for the kingdom of God. The scriptures tell us: *"Then the king commanded, and they brought Daniel, and cast **him** into the den of lions. Now the king spake and said unto Daniel, Thy God whom thou servest continually, <u>he will deliver thee</u>. And a stone was brought, and laid upon the mouth of the den; and the king sealed it with his own signet, and with the signet of his lords; that the purpose might not be changed concerning Daniel." (Daniel 6:16-17)*

As king Darius gave the order concerning Daniel, so it was carried out. His heart was not to see Daniel killed, but he also had fallen into the trap of deception, being deceived by his own counselors and lords. Now he was feeling the regret of having signed the writing, and seeing his most loyal subject sentenced to death by his own mistake. But even in his own ignorance of the trap that had been set for him, he still spoke to Daniel a word of faith, knowing and believing that his God could deliver him, and believing that Daniels God could work a great miracle. If this godless king could believe that Daniels' God could deliver him, how much more should we believe our Lord for our deliverance?! How much more should we believe Him for our salvation, our healing, our sanctification and deliverance? Many times, the unbelieving seem to have more faith than we have; but we must shake ourselves and know that our God will deliver us.

The torture of being cast alive into a den of hungry lions was the punishment for Daniel devised by his enemies. They wanted to see him destroyed, not just hurt, but dead. The enemy wants to destroy us, especially when we stand against him for the kingdom of God's sake. And he will fight against us with all his wiles to do what he can to harm us. We can see his works alive and well now working to destroy God's people with all force. It is true that the devil is come with wrath knowing he has but a short time. He won't stop at anything until he brings death and destruction if possible. The way of escape that we have is the blood of Jesus that keeps us and helps us through all that we might face. His blood will never lose its power, but is all powerful and able to conquer any obstacle.

The roar of accusation against Daniel was now followed by the hungry ferocious roar of real lions in a den that were waiting and ready to devour any prey given to them. King Darius lords' took no time to do exactly what they had planned, taking Daniel and casting him into the lions' den. Daniel, no doubt, knew what was facing him as he was cast alive into a dark den full of lions' that were preparing for the kill. Daniel's faith and trust in God were going to be tested as never before, and it would have to be the Lord to deliver him and set him free from this trap. We can't imagine what fear might have gripped Daniel's heart as he saw the ferocious beasts lurking toward him, ready to attack the fresh prey set before them. Snarls, roars, we don't know all that Daniel saw and heard; but as a child of God he didn't allow what he was seeing and hearing bring fear to his heart, but looked up to heaven knowing his God was faithful.

As Daniel was cast into the den, the enemy thought he had the battle won, but he forgets that the God we serve is aware of his devices. Even so when the enemy roars against us, he can think that he has won the battle, and that we will not be delivered from his hand. We must know that our God will deliver us, and **shut the lion's mouth!**

The Lord's mighty hand of protection was ready to receive Daniel as he fell into the den of lions, and he had an angel prepared to meet Daniel in the bottom of that den. We can imagine Daniel in the midst of ferocious lions surrounding him, praising and worshipping the Lord, and blessing the God of his salvation! **Our God delivers again and again!!**

Look at your life right now – you may be facing a den full of spiritual lions that seem to be ready to devour and destroy you. The enemy has set the trap that was used to pull you into a place of false accusation, trying your faith, your patience, and your will. Not knowing how things are going to work out, we many times fret about the unknown, and doubts and fears can grip our hearts. But we must look up to heaven, calling upon Jesus and knowing that he will deliver us from all evil. The divine providence of our Heavenly Father knows and sees all things, and his provision will keep us even when the enemy seems to have the victory over us. The Lord will not allow us to be pressed above what we are able, and always will make a way to escape the temptation. There are times we would like to avoid these kinds of trials if possible, but it is better for us to be tried with the Lord on our side, than for everything to be going great and not have the Lord on our side. So when the devil roars against your life, trying to tear you apart by his wicked devices, know that the Lord is faithful to deliver you out of his hand. He may have your back against the wall, but this is the Lord's greatest hour, and He shows his mighty hand by sending us deliverance!

As we have read, king Darius, knowing Daniel's true innocence, even told Daniel that he knew his God would deliver him. The king passed that night fasting, not knowing how this would all turn out. The night seemed endless, as hour by hour passed, and the king no doubt pacing the floor. Not being able to sleep, he went early that morning to the den of lions. As he approached the den, the silence of the den could have made him believe that Daniel was dead, and that the lions surely had destroyed him. But in his lamentable voice he cried out to Daniel:

"O Daniel, servant of the living God, is thy God, whom thou servest continually, able to deliver thee from the lions?"(Daniel 6:20)

It seemed as though the seconds of silence were an eternity, but then the silence was broken by Daniel's victorious voice as he answered, *"O king, live forever. My God hath sent his angel and <u>hath shut the lions' mouths</u>, that they have not hurt me: forasmuch as before him innocency was found in me; and also before thee, o king, have I done no hurt."(v.21-22)*

What? Can we believe that this man Daniel, who was cast alive into a den of live, flesh eating lions all night long, was alive and well enough to answer the king when he called? Oh yes, what glorious, miraculous victory came to a man of God who stood the test of faith, and did not bow to the kings' edict, even at the risk of losing his life! How many of us could stand a test as great as this? We have read of Daniel in the lions' den since we were children in Sunday school, saw pictures and drawings of this Bible story, but little do we realize the reality of an ugly lions' roar against us to destroy our very lives if possible. The same God that sent an angel to meet Daniel at the bottom of the den of lions, is the same Lord that will send his Holy Ghost to meet us at our darkest hour; when the devil is closing in for the kill, he sends the Comforter to help us to rejoice in battle, and see the victory won!

We have many people that contact us for prayer for the many needs in their lives. They share their situations with us, and some accounts of the events of their lives are almost unbelievable. Even as we are living in physically perilous times, the spiritual peril far outweighs anything that we encounter in the flesh.

Spiritual warfare is being waged against every child of God: churches, pastors, ministries – attacked with no mercy and not a way to seem to escape. But fear not! The one who knows how to shut the lion's mouth is here to fight for us, and bring us through the ugliest of situations that we could ever face. We must know and be confident that God's word is true, and His promises are sure, and he will not fail us.

We can't fail to think that Daniel didn't cry out to his Heavenly Father for help. In the darkness of the den of lions, beholding the glare of many eyes looking at him, he used the tool that he knew would get him an answer: PRAYER!! And when he did, something miraculous happened in that cold dark den of death! **God shut the lion's mouth!!** Praise Jesus for his delivering power! Halleluiah! And He will do the same for us today! Don't fear; know that what he has done before, he can do it again for you!

King Darius, in his excitement, commanded Daniel to be brought up out of the den, and Daniel came forth without any hurt or harm. The king then commanded Daniels accusers, their wives and children, all to be cast into the den of lions. They were killed as soon as they reached the bottom of the den, which shows us that truly the Lord makes a difference for His people. The protection that Daniel had was not there to defend those that had accused him and desired his death. Instead, death took them and their families, truly displaying the results of sin! Sin always brings death, but for the believer, the gift of God is eternal life through Jesus Christ our Lord! The scripture says that *"There shall no evil befall thee, neither shall any plague come nigh thy dwelling."* It also says *"a thousand shall fall at thy side and ten thousand at thy right hand, but it shall not come nigh thee." (Psalm 91:7, 10)* Thank God for his wonderful promises of protection and help, and the hope that he will always deliver us!

King Darius was so amazed at the mighty power of Daniels' God, that he wrote a decree to all people:

He wrote, *"I make a decree, That in every dominion of my kingdom men tremble and fear before the God of Daniel: for he is the living God, and stedfast for ever, and his kingdom that which shall not be destroyed, and his dominion shall be even unto the end. He delivereth and rescueth, and he worketh signs and wonders in heaven and in earth, who hath delivered Daniel from the power of the lions." (Daniel 6:26-27)*

King Darius spoke the truth concerning Daniels' God, knowing that no idol or image could deliver someone as Daniel had been delivered. He recognized the power of the true living God, and understood that His power is incomparable, reaching far beyond the greatest kings and kingdoms, and the surpassing understanding of the wisest of that time. How great a revival would come if our governing leaders would make this same discovery, realizing that our God is God, and that his son Jesus is the only way to heaven! If they could only realize who Jesus is and that He came to deliver us in miraculous ways, it would surely turn the hearts of the people back to the Lord.

The God of Daniel is the same God that has delivered us many times out of the mouth of the lion, and we must continue to believe him, as even this king said, that all nations and kingdoms would fear and tremble before him. There are many things that people fear in these days, and many precautions are taken to uphold our physical lives and liberty. But the spiritual life is pushed into the background and forgotten, and the same devil that roared against Daniel in those days is roaring against man's soul, seeking to devour and destroy. Unfortunately he succeeds, because man fails to turn to the Lord, and is devoured by the enemy into eternity without the Lord, as a lost soul bound for eternal destruction. But there is a mighty God in heaven, and His Son Jesus has paid the price for us; a price that could not be paid by another, and we can be redeemed by His precious blood, and delivered out of the mouth of the lion. Whether the enemy rages through temptation, trial, persecution, false accusations, or any other means, our Lord is still greater in power and might, and he will pull down the strongholds of the enemy. Remember, the weapons of our warfare are not carnal, but mighty through God!

In closing this chapter, our plea goes out to those that will hear today. If we all would find the faith and courage to take a stand as Daniel did, even in the face of certain death, and hold onto our spiritual integrity.

We must uphold the Christian values that we know our nation was founded upon. As ministers and leaders of the church, if we would pray as Daniel prayed, fight for our rights and freedoms to gather, pray, and worship as the Lord commands us, we will see the changes come that are so desperately needed. In this desperate hour, we need to be that desperate people, seeking after King Jesus, and knowing that His soon return is imminent. Let faith arise in our hearts as never before, seeing that beautiful beatitude that said, *"Blessed are they which are persecuted for righteousness sake; for theirs' is the kingdom of heaven." (Matthew 5:12)* Prepare your hearts, for He is coming soon!

"And what shall I more say? for the time would fail me to tell of Gedeon, and of Barak, and of Samson, and of Jephthae; of David also, and Samuel, and of the prophets: Who through faith subdued kingdoms, wrought righteousness, obtained promises, <u>stopped the mouths of lions,</u> Quenched the violence of fire, escaped the edge of the sword, out of weakness were made strong, waxed valiant in fight, turned to flight the armies of the aliens. Women received their dead raised to life again: and others were tortured, not accepting deliverance; that they might obtain a better resurrection:"

(Hebrews 11:32-35)

CHAPTER SIX:
JESUS–KING OF KINGS & LORD OF LORDS!
THE CONQUERER OF ALL!

"These shall make war with the Lamb, and the Lamb shall overcome them: for he is Lord of lords, and King of kings:"
(Rev. 17:14)

Through the last several chapters, we have discussed many different characters, some who faithfully stood the test as spiritual lions of adversity roared against them, and some who fell into the trap of deception and sin, as Satan roared against them through the wiles of deception. But in this last chapter will look to the greatest of all our spiritual examples, the Author and Finisher of our faith: the one who for the joy set before Him, endured the cross, despised the shame, and is set down at the right hand of the majesty on high! Our JESUS, Emmanuel, our God with us! What a blessed redeemer we serve. In a divine body prepared for Him, He came, sent from the Father above to mankind, as redeemer, restorer, and life giver to those who would believe upon His wonderful name! There's not another name like the name of our Jesus! There is no other name given under heaven whereby we can be saved! To Him belongs all the praise and glory for being our sacrifice, and by Him we are able to live, preach, and teach his wonderful word that speaks life into us.

God sent His Son in the likeness of sinful flesh and for sin, to live, preach, teach, heal the sick, raise the dead: He then gave His divine blood for us on

Calvary, rose again from the dead, and gave us the promise of eternal life, with the promise of the Comforter, the Holy Ghost to give us power over all the power of the devil. This completed and fulfilled the God's plan of salvation, the Gospel as we know it: to deliver the soul of man from the judgment of death, hell and damnation. How thankful we should be that Jesus paid it all for us, and truly delivered us from the mouth of a raging lion that wanted every soul of man destroyed. Satan's plan was to separate us from God, and bring spiritual death to mankind. But God so loved us, that He had a different plan. He sent His very best, his only begotten Son, His pure and holy Son from heaven, to be our Redeemer. In doing so Jesus fulfilled the prophecies that told of his suffering, death, and resurrection hundreds of years before, proving that He was the true Messiah, our Savior! Even Daniel, the prophet we just studied in the last chapter gave many prophecies concerning the Lord Jesus. In this chapter we will study some of these great prophecies, and see that Jesus is our greatest example: and how he overcame and conquered our spiritual enemy, Satan and the Devil that roared against him as a lion!

Being our great Redeemer and our great High Priest, Jesus went through the toils of living a life in the flesh; he felt, knew, and understood the infirmities of the fleshly life, so that He could bear the burdens of mankind, giving us the power to overcome this life. Being without sin or guile, the devil had to use many different means to roar against him, as he tried to stop the plan of God any way he could. He didn't want Jesus to give His life for man's sin; it would destroy and spoil his plans to keep man separated from God, and lost for eternity. As we will read, the Lord was able to conquer, and fulfill the plan of God giving us this great salvation.

We are going to begin with the beautiful prophecies concerning Christ Jesus in Psalm twenty-two. This chapter gives to us another prophetic look into the life of Christ and his time of suffering, and is very detail specific, following along with prophecies written in the book of Isaiah chapter fifty three. King David, whom is attributed as the author of this Psalm, had a glorious vision of the Son of Gods' sufferings. Some have said that these were some of David's own sufferings; but the great many details which were fulfilled by Jesus at the cross of Calvary lead us to know that they were prophetic words inspired by the Holy Ghost, as these words were written and fulfilled by the Lord. Even King David was promised that from his seed, the Savior would come. We believe that David was inspired to write these words, and show us what great love that our Savior and Redeemer would give to us through his great sacrifice. It is revealed by the scriptures that *"it behoved Christ to suffer, and to rise from the dead the third day:" (Luke 24:46)*

The sufferings that Jesus endured are the foundation of the Gospel; from his betrayal, trial, judgment, crucifixion, his death and burial, we find so many Bible prophecies he fulfilled to the exact detail. As we study these glorious prophecies, we pray it would make every unbelieving person in this world retract their scoffs of unbelief when they read and hear the incredible evidence given to us in Bible prophecy concerning the Lord Jesus. To the natural man it is only a matter of coincidence, not having what they say is substantial proof to be true. But to the spiritual man, by faith we believe these prophecies to be true, and know that they were fulfilled by the Lord Jesus Christ. Most of all, they have been fulfilled in us who believe that Jesus is the Son of God, and through his sufferings, He shed His divine blood that was the atonement for our sins. Our faith in His promises has changed our lives, giving us a new life in Christ Jesus. Through that faith in these prophetic words, we have seen victory come in our lives. His Word gives us victory over the unending roar of that spiritual lion that wants to keep us from making heaven our home. It also gives us the hope that we will see Jesus one day very soon, as He returns for His bride! So with all we are and all the strength we have, we've got to make it, and we can do all things through Christ which strengthens us! Thank you Jesus!

Before we discuss the 22nd chapter of Psalms, we would like to look at what Jesus had to face in the hours leading up to His sacrifice on the cross. His disciples had gathered for the Passover meal, and made preparation as the Lord had commanded them. During this supper, the Lord Jesus made the announcement that one at the table would betray him. Of course the reaction was overwhelming: Lord, who is it that will betray you?! Many denied and pledged to never betray him. But Satan had entered into the heart of Judas Iscariot, and planted the seed of betrayal and deception in his soul. Jesus was not blinded by this fact, and realizing it was Judas, He told him, *"that thou doest, do quickly."* (John 13:27) Judas left into the stillness of the dark night, alone, being led by a Satan's spirit tormenting him to betray the Son of God. This was the plan of God being fulfilled, and Jesus realizing His hour had come, He began to encourage the other disciples with a beautiful discourse of words that would ring in their hearts forever. Jesus gave His word to us as he spoke to his disciples with words of encouragement: *"Let not your heart be troubled; ye believe in God, believe also in me."(John 14:1) "I am the way the truth and the life; no man cometh unto the Father but by me."(John 14:6)* Again he told them, *"we will come unto him, and make our abode with him."(John 14:23),* speaking of the Holy Ghost whom the Father would send in His name as the Comforter.

Though the ugly deceptive spirit of betrayal was roaring against him, he never once regarded the welfare of his own life, but looked to the good of those disciples whom he loved and had ministered unto. He wanted to know that their joy would be full, and that even in the sorrow of His departing, the Comforter would come to them and lead and guide them into all truth.

What a glorious Savior we serve, that came not to be ministered unto, but said, " *Even as the Son of man came not to be ministered unto, but to minister, and to give his life a ransom for many.*" (Matthew 20:28) He came to pay the ransom for our souls! That should cause us to appreciate the Lord so much! The perils of the flesh, the fear of betrayal and death looming never once caused him to shutter or be dismayed, though he realized he would face this battle alone.

Through His great example we understand that when these trials come, we are not to fear or be dismayed: *"For God hath not given us the spirit of fear, but of power, and love, and of a sound mind."*(2 Timothy 1:7) Jesus was the perfect example of fearless love, having his heart and mind set to do his Father's will. So we must take this example and know that we can also overcome. Even when betrayal, conflict, deception and lies are all around, and the enemy is roaring nonstop to destroy our joy, we can still have peace to the fullest in the presence of the Lord.

After the supper and discourse with His disciples, Jesus led the disciples to the garden to pray. This time of prayer was going to be the most important. The battle for the souls of mankind was going to take place at Gethsemane, the mount of Olives where Jesus would resort to pray. Knowing the hour had come, He had to have the communion of His Father to carry him through the hours of temptation and trial that lay ahead. Gethsemane is actually translated from the Greek as "olive press". It was the place where he was to be "crushed" to bring life once again for mankind, and salvation for our eternal souls.

As He began to feel the load and weight of what he was going to face, and the suffering he was going to endure, he told his disciples to "w*atch and pray, that ye enter not into temptation: the spirit indeed is willing, but the flesh is weak." (Matthew 26:41)* His words of strength were to encourage the disciples at a time when he truly needed strength and help to endure. The weight of the sin of the entire world, every sickness, every disease was coming upon him, to be crucified and atoned for on an old rugged cross. What an emblem of suffering and shame! Jesus, the precious spotless Lamb of God bore it all for us, and sometimes we have difficulty with the trials that we have to face. We can never imagine what a load the Son of God carried for us to the cross. He was being crushed under the load and burden of sin. The scripture in Isaiah 53:4 says, *"Surely he hath borne our griefs and carried our sorrows, yet we did esteem him stricken, smitten of God and afflicted."* Those words *"he hath borne"* in the Hebrew text are actually in the sense of taking a load from someone's shoulders and putting it on their own. It imitates as a mother bearing a child! Can we see what Jesus did for us? Can we understand that He took it from us, so that we don't have to bear it! Not only sorrow, but sin, sickness, disease, infirmities of the flesh: He bore it all for us. Isaiah repeats in verse eleven of the same chapter: *"for he shall bear their iniquities."* What great love and mercy He has shown us by what He did for us. Please take advantage of the opportunity He gave to us by turning your life completely to Jesus.

Many fail the Lord in trying times because they can't bear the crushing of the flesh, and the putting away of the carnal man. But Jesus knew He must go through, and what He set his mind to do. Not only was He feeling the weight of the sin of the entire world, but also the powers of hell that were waging war against him in the garden as he prayed. Satan's entire armies of demonic power and principalities were waging a war, and that raging lion was roaring as the battle was being fought there in the garden as Jesus prayed. The disciples were fallen to sleep as sorrow had filled their hearts, and fear of the unknown future. But for Jesus, his heart was broken under the load and burden He was carrying. The scriptures tell us: *"And he took with him Peter and the two sons of Zebedee, and began to be sorrowful and very heavy. Then saith he unto them, <u>My soul is exceeding sorrowful, even unto death:</u> tarry ye here, and watch with me. And he went a little further, and <u>fell on his face</u>, and prayed, saying, O my Father, if it be possible, let this cup pass from me: nevertheless not as I will, but as thou wilt." (Matthew 26:37-39)* The account in the Gospel of Luke is similar, but adds something very important: *"And he was withdrawn from them about a stone's cast, and kneeled down, and prayed, Saying, Father, if thou be willing, remove this cup from me: nevertheless not my will, but thine, be done. And there appeared an angel unto him from heaven, strengthening him. And being in an agony he prayed more earnestly: and his sweat was as it were great drops of blood falling down to the ground. (Luke 22:41-44)*

The agonizing cry of the Son of God to our Heavenly Father is what gained him the strength to overcome and go through this terrible test of suffering unto death. The word *"agony"* is translated from the Greek meaning *"a struggle"* and *"to compete for a prize, to* contend *with an adversary, fight, labor fervently"*. As we read in these scriptures that His agony was so great, His sweat was as it were great drops of blood falling to the ground. There have been recorded cases in which, through mental pressure, the pores may be so dilated that the blood may issue from them; so that there may be a bloody sweat. We can be certain that Jesus felt this pressure being in such agony; and being pushed to the limit. The weight was overwhelming for the natural man, but being the Son of God full of the Holy Ghost, He was still the victorious Son of God against the enemies' ever tormenting roars of death! The devil and his armies were roaring against Him fiercely, attempting to stop Him from going to the cross for us. But Jesus knew His Father's will must be accomplished, and He would not fail to keep His promise.

Even so, we are given the power to stand against the wiles of the devil and his threatening roars of fear and unbelief; not knowing the outcome of situations, but knowing that the Lord is faithful to see us through. The writer in Hebrews speaks of Jesus saying, *"Who in the days of his flesh, when he had offered up prayers and supplications with strong crying and tears unto him that was able to save him from death, and was heard in that he feared; Though he were a Son, yet learned he obedience by the things which he suffered; And being made perfect, he became the author of eternal salvation unto all them that obey him; (Hebrews 5:7-9)*

There are many great secrets in these scriptures: keys to help us to be victorious against the roars of satanic powers that come against us. Jesus knew that His strength could be found in prayer unto God. As we studied in the previous chapter of the importance of a prayer life for every child of God, once again we stress the importance of having our communication with our Heavenly Father at all times. Our spiritual strength comes through the Holy Ghost as He ministers to us in our prayer life. Jesus was heard as he prayed in agony through strong crying and tears, and received the strength he needed in that hour.

Are you in a valley of trial and testing, and not sure of what to do or which way to go? In agony, find yourself on your knees before the Lord, knowing that if we cry unto him He will hear us and answer! Jesus even fell on his face, as the agony of the hour was weighing heavy upon him. But power from on high came as our heavenly Father heard him, and answered.

The next point we know is key to our success in living for the Lord in these perilous times. We must be willing to submit to God's will for our lives. Though Jesus was and is the Son of God, He still learned "obedience" – the scripture says, by the things which he suffered. The situation turned when he spoke those words, and said *"Nevertheless, not my will but thine be done"*. Whatever the outcome, whatever the answer, it must be God's will in all things. This is where we learn our obedience to the Lord, even in situations of which we suffer. Through submission, humility, and suffering, Jesus became our Author of Eternal Salvation! The greatest gift given to man was God's only Son, and He is our Lord today because of His obedience to His Father. Now we must be obedient, submitted to the will of God, and faithful to fulfill His every command. As we obey Him and His word, we are made His children, heirs of the great promises of the Bible.

Now Jesus was ready to go through the most difficult of all battles, as all the raging lions of hell were roaring against Him, doing anything possible thinking they could destroy the Son of God. He found the strength He needed, and as he was tried before the

Jews and before Pilate, he fulfilled the sacred words written by the prophet Isaiah hundreds of years before: *"He was oppressed, and he was afflicted, yet he opened not his mouth: he is brought as a lamb to the slaughter, and as a sheep before her shearers is dumb, so he openeth not his mouth."(Isaiah 53:7)*

In complete and total submission to God, humble as a sheep before the shearer, as a lamb led to the slaughter, he didn't fight back in vengeance, but took the place of every guilty sinner from the beginning of creation, and carried our sin to the cross in His body. This is the wonderful Savior that we serve, who didn't think of himself, but wanted to please His Father and lay down His life for us that we might live and not die. That is why we owe Him everything! He paid a debt He did not owe! Even when the roars of false accusation, the roars of pain and affliction, the roars of suffering never seen in mortal man before, Jesus didn't hesitate, He paid it all! In His innocence and purity, he became the one and only true sacrifice for mans' sins, and we are saved today because of what He has done for us. If Jesus had not come to die for us, the world as we know it would be lost: we would have no opportunity for salvation and eternal life, and judgment surely would have taken man to eternal destruction. But His sacrifice, His suffering, His pain was not in vain. Through those sufferings and by His precious blood that was shed, those who believe and serve Him now have the hope of eternal life in Jesus!

As He was crucified, the prophetic words from Psalm Twenty-two were fulfilled through the suffering which he endured. From the beginning of the Psalm, there are many scriptures that were fulfilled as Jesus suffered on the cross. The scriptures tell us: *"**Many bulls have compassed me: strong bulls of Bashan have beset me round. They gaped upon me with their mouths, as a ravening and a roaring lion.** I am poured out like water, and all my bones are out of joint: my heart is like wax; it is melted in the midst of my bowels. My strength is dried up like a potsherd; and my tongue cleaveth to my jaws; and thou hast brought me into the dust of death. For dogs have compassed me: the assembly of the wicked have inclosed me: they pierced my hands and my feet. I may tell all my bones: they look and stare upon me. They part my garments among them, and cast lots upon my vesture."* (Psalm 22:12-18)

As if the brutal pain and shame of the cross was not enough to bare, the enemies of the Lord despitefully mocked him as he was suffering unto death. These prophetic words tell us of the mockery and abuse he received while on the cross. These wicked spiritual lions that had deceived and lied to see him crucified opened their mouths wide to roar and devour what bit of life might be left in His body. After being tried, scourged, platted with a crown of thorns, nailed to the tree, what more could be done to inflict undue and unmerciful pain upon him? It was a terrible sight to behold, unimaginable to the human mind.

As Pilate told the Jews "Behold the man". Isaiah prophesied and said, *"his visage was so marred more than any man, and his form more than the sons of men:"(Isaiah 52:14)* It was the most severe hardship, the signs of agony and distress. Pain was only a small part of what the Savior endured, and the signs of his sufferings marred his very appearance. In the crucifixion he became acquainted with grief, pain, hunger, thirst, fatigue, the greatest weight of sorrows laid upon him. His bones pained with the inflicted nails in his hands and feet, and His mind suffered with the weight of the worlds' sin, sickness, and disease. These were marks of a criminal laid upon the innocent, unjustly inflicted wounds that were not deserved. They gambled for the robe that he wore, not realizing what they were doing. Yet he took it for you, he took it for all of us. Behold His face! Think upon His distressed nerves, weary limbs, aching head, wounded spirit, and broken heart! We then can understand the reality of His work. God might have left us to our fate, bound for judgment and death; but where would then have been the glory of His grace? He might have forgiven us and saved us with a word; but where then would have been the purity of His holiness, justice, and truth? Sin had to be tried, judged, condemned, and atoned for: and only Jesus, the Son of God was worthy to be that sacrifice for us today.

Why would it be that people so easily despise and turn away his grace today? What would cause a person to read these blessed scriptures, knowing what the Savior did for us, and walk away unchanged, uncaring, rejecting the great love that God has shown to mankind through the gift of His Son Jesus? It can only be the blindness of the heart, the idolatry of self-worship, pride, and the love of the world and the world system. These are only a few examples of how Satan has roared, as a roaring lion, devouring whom he may to keep them from the promise of eternal life. We must see Jesus, the great love He showed to us on the cross, the suffering and shame he endured to bring us to promise of eternal life. And through His death He gave us the victory over sin at Calvary! What a miracle He has done in our lives! Sin does not have to reign over us! The roars of temptation do not have to overcome us, but we can overcome them through the blood of the Lamb!

The devil roared against Jesus, and thought he had the victory won when Jesus died on the cross. As Joseph and the others carried his body to the sepulcher, the silent roars of sorrow, grief, doubt and unbelief covered their minds with a cloud of discouragement. The disciples hearts were filled with sorrow as the Lord had told them, and the fears of what would happen next took them into hiding. Satan surely believed he had the battle won, but this war was not over. Those precious words the Lord spoke as he gave us His life for us; "It is finished" – were words of terror to the ruthless enemy that roared against the Son of God in death. Jesus finished the work at Calvary, defeated Satan, and atoned for the sins of mankind by the blood which He shed. Now, Satan was a defeated foe, and the veil of the temple rent in two giving us access to the throne of His mighty grace! Amazing Grace, how sweet the sound; that saved a wretch like me! We once were lost, but now we are found, we were blind but now we see!

On the third day, early that morning, something happened that was more than supernatural. The Lord had promised his disciples that after three days He would rise again; and just as he promised, so did he fulfill. The roars of death and the grave seemed to have his body bound in a tomb, unable to be helped by any mortal man. The silence of a dark sealed tomb seemed to be the end of the story. It seemed a hopeless situation to the flesh, and seemed to be so final. The devil has ways of making us think that situations are hopeless, but Jesus came to change all of that. A preacher once said that Jesus took the "T" out of can't, and made it "CAN" to let us know no matter how difficult or impossible things may look, our God is a God of the impossible!

With the mighty thundering of an earthquake, an angel came and rolled the stone back from the sepulcher. All the powers of death, hell and the grave were shattered as the Father called His Son from the grave! The roars of death were silenced as the Son of God came forth in the newness of life, His resurrected body glorified by the victory over the grave and death! God truly *"shut the lion's mouth"* and the roars of Satan and the sting of death could no longer touch Him. The victory was taken from the grave and given to the Son of God Jesus, O blessed be His name forever! With all authority and power Jesus arose, alive to give to all who would believe the same promise of eternal life! Then we rejoice in the scripture that says, *"O death, where is thy sting? O grave, where is thy victory?!"* This fulfillment of prophecy gave us the hope of that glorious resurrection that the Lord has promised to us. If we had no hope of the resurrection, we would surely be men most miserable! But thank the Lord today that we have a hope beyond this life, and that one day, our glorious Savior Jesus Christ shall return again to take us home to be with him forever.

As Jesus told John the Apostle in the book of Revelation: *"Fear not; I am the first and the last: I am he that liveth, and was dead; and, behold, I am alive for evermore, Amen; and have the keys of hell and of death. (Revelation 1:7-8)* There is not a power in hell that can stand against the mighty Son of God; He is alive and holds the keys of death, hell and the grave! And praise God that He has given us the same victory through our salvation over death and the power of the grave!

Now, because of the victory Jesus brought to us through His resurrection, we can reverse the situation, and look to "THE LION OF THE TRIBE OF JUDAH", the one who stepped forth to take victory over Satan and His devices. As the angel told

John in Revelation that *"the lion of the tribe of Juda, the root of David, hath prevailed"!* Our great King of Kings and Lord of Lords that is coming back to save and deliver us from the perils of this life, and He is the one who can conquer and overcome any situation that we may face.

In closing, we would like to encourage everyone that reads to take hold of the promises of God, and know that through His Word we can overcome any spiritual lion that roars against us. This study only has a few examples of those that overcame, and the means given to them to make them victorious over the enemy. What Jesus did for us on the cross is proof enough that we don't have to yield to the threats of the enemy but stand against him in victory. The war is being waged against us to destroy every soul, every life, and if possible, the lives of those whom we love. We must stand against the wiles of the devil, take the authority Jesus gave us in the scriptures to not only overcome that roaring lion, but cast him out and let him know that he is not welcome in our homes, our families, our churches, even in our nation. Is there hope of deliverance from this wicked enemy that roars against the church? Oh yes there is!!

"And the devil that deceived them was cast into the lake of fire and brimstone, where the beast and the false prophet are, and shall be tormented day and night for ever and ever." (Revelation 20:10)